After much research, however, I have concluded that the dates offered by Rumi  Shams vary, and none can precise. Therefore, for th tion the year and the mo sible, and omit the day. As for the transliteration of the Persian words, I have preferred to use the Persian pronunciation versus Arabic or Turkish, using the Iranian Studies transliteration scheme; and where certain words are already known and accepted in English, I have used that spelling.

EARLY YEARS

Mohammad, son of Ali, son of Malekdâd, known as Shams ed-Din, was born in Tabriz, the present capital of the Iranian province of Azarbaijân, in 1184 (Sâheb-Zamâni 1990, 107). Shams, which in Arabic means "the sun" (Shams ed-Din means "the sun of faith"), was the only son of a shopkeeper father who adored him and raised him with utmost care. From very early on, Shams showed signs of being different from other boys. He preferred his own company to that of others his age and hardly ever engaged in childhood games, preferring to spend his time with his books.

Shams's father had high hopes for his son and had him study Arabic, Islamic law, mathematics, and astronomy with the most learned teachers available. It is believed that by the age of seven, Shams had already begun to memorize the Koran, and not long after, he knew it by heart, becoming a hâfez. We know a fair amount about Shams's early life, unlike most other Sufis of his time, because here and there he mentions his family in his *Maghâlât*. These *Discourses*, which we will discuss at length later, were roughly scribed by a *morīd*, or devotee, who was privy to Shams's talks, and they are our most valid source of information on Shams.

Shams describes his father as a kind and emotional man whose tears were easily drawn. He imparts almost no information on his mother, though, her personality being immersed into his father's. In one instance, he speaks of how delicately and lovingly his parents raised him, yet at the same time, he criticizes them, as in the following instance in which he implies how exasperating his father's kindness to a cat that had tried to steal their food is. In those days, people were not generally well off, and meat was not a staple of their diets; in fact, it was a luxury and a real treat. It was common that when meat was being served in a meal, the local cats would quickly gather, waiting for their chance to pounce on it.

> If a cat spilled and broke a bowl trying to steal the meat, my father, sitting next to me with his stick by his side, would never hit the animal and would jokingly say: "Look how she's done it again! This is good fortune! We've been spared from evil. Otherwise something bad could've happened to either you, me, or your mother!" (Movahed 2009, 173)

In his teens, Shams began to experience unusual mental states, which was a source of worry for his parents. These curious moods were invigorated when he began to attend and serve as a novice in *samâ* (whirling ceremonies), experimenting with Sufism and its various spiritual practices. These experiences would strongly affect his temperament as well as his physical constitution, especially his dietary habits: at times he would lose his appetite completely, unable to even swallow properly. His sleep also became minimal, yet he felt energized and stronger than ever. In his own words:

> My appetite has been eradicated by "discourse"; three or four days pass without me feeling any hunger. And my father says: "My poor son, nothing passes through his lips!" But I tell him that I don't become any weaker, and my power is such that if you wish to see it I could fly to the sun like a bird. (Movahed 2009, *Khomi az Sharab e Rabani*, 222)

Shams's poor father ceaselessly worried for him, unaware of what was becoming of his beloved only child. He would ask Shams:

> "What is happening to you?"
> "Nothing has happened to me! Do I look mad? Have I torn someone's clothes off his back? Have I picked a fight with you?"
> "Then what is this state I find you in? I know that you're not mad, but I don't understand what you're doing, my son!" (Movahed 2009, 223)

Ali ibn-e Malekdâd, Shams's father, was familiar with the common Sufi practices of the time, because Tabriz was known as the City of Seventy Bâbâs (fathers), a term referring to shaykhs (Arabic), *morsheds*, and *pīrs* (Persian), or Sufi mentors and masters. Shams's condition, however, was unlike that of most Sufis and baffled his father, who would worry himself sick as he watched his son wither away.

Shams says of his father: "He was a good man . . . but he wasn't a lover. A good man is one thing and a lover is another. . . . Only a lover can know about the state of another lover" (Movahed 1997, 44). For Shams to be in love was to be burning in the fire of love all the time.

The relationship between father and son gradually but steadily deteriorated, and as Shams began to realize how different he was from his kin, his father's kindness began to seem intrusive and even hostile at times. He says, "My father had no notion about me. I was a stranger in my own town, and my father was becoming a stranger to me. I was more estranged every day and began to think that even when he spoke kindly and paternally to me, in fact he preferred to beat me and throw me out of his house!" (Movahed 2009, 223).

Shams's feelings of alienation, however, did not affect his self-confidence or his belief in his own spiritual powers. He tells of an exchange with his father:

> I told him, let me tell you just one thing! The way you are with me is like duck eggs that have been left under a hen. The eggs eventually hatch and the

ducklings instinctively walk to the stream. They slide into the water and swim away, as their mother, a domestic hen, only walks alongside them on the bank, without the prospect of ever getting into the water herself. Father, I can now see that the sea has become my carrier, my home! This is the real state of my being. If you are from me and me from you, then come into the sea; otherwise, you can bide your time with the hens in their coop. (Movahed 2009, *Shams e Tabrizi*, 44)

Elsewhere in the *Maghâlât*, Shams reiterates his feelings about his father:

If it weren't for Mowlânâ I would never have returned to Konya. . . . Had they brought me the news that my father had risen from the grave and sent me a message to go and see him and come back to Damascus with him, I would never have even considered going! (Movahed 2009, 77)

SHAMS'S SUFI INITIATION

Seeing no other choice, Ali ibn-e Malekdâd had to let his teenage son join Shaykh Abu Bakr Seleh-Bâf in his independent *khâneghâh,* a Sufi house, in the Charandâb quarter in Tabriz. Shams describes his *pīr* as a soul who was indifferent to the "Lords of Power and Gold." Every time members of the government wished to pay their respects, the shaykh's students would exaggerate their acts of devotion to their teacher, excessively bowing and keeping their distance with their hands crossed over their hearts, intending to belittle the wealthy visitors.

Shams seems to have adopted Shaykh Abu Bakr's indifference to wealth and authority, in addition to relinquishing the popular custom of taking part in special Sufi ceremonies. In the Sufi tradition, it is common for shaykhs to initiate their *morīd* upon the completion of their studies by giving them a *khergheh,* the cloak of a *darvish.* Shams, however, insisted that it was not Abu Bakr's practice to bestow a *khergheh,* thus emphasizing the fact that he did not adhere to common Sufi rituals. Many years later, Shams was asked to reveal his own *khergheh* and to introduce his own shaykh, to prove that he was a genuinely initiated *darvish,* and he cunningly replied:

> The Prophet, peace be upon him, has gifted me my *khergheh* in my sleep! And it's not one of those that

ages after two days and ends up in tatters only fit to clean toilets with; but it's a robe of "teaching," teachings that cannot be comprehended by everyone, teachings that do not belong to yesterday or tomorrow. What can love possibly have to do with yesterday and tomorrow anyway? (Movahed 1997, 62)

At the time when Shams was growing up in Tabriz, the two main Islamic schools that the people of Azarbaijân belonged to were the Hanafi and Shafi'i, which was a major source of contention and animosity between the inhabitants. Shams belonged to the Shafi'i school, but unlike most conservative Hanafis, who generally disparaged Shafi'i principles, Shams as a Shafi'i was himself open to Hanafi principles when he found them useful. Later on in life, he would refute fanaticism by teaching and practicing tolerance in his daily life and encouraging acceptance and camaraderie between the various factions in Islam, an outlook that he later transferred to Rumi, who belonged to the Hanafi school.

In his youth, Shams had studied Islamic jurisprudence and had learned the Koran by heart, studying under the religious authorities of his time. As a young man, however, when he first became attracted to Sufism and the practices of the *darvishes,* he shunned the mullahs, believing that they had no concept of mysticism. As time went by and he mingled with *darvishes,* he came to believe that perhaps spending time with the mullahs was more honest than wasting time with fraudulent, useless, and freeloading mystics, who were abundant and who showed no trace of spirituality in their lives. In Shams's own words:

> At first I did not mingle with the religious scholars, only with *darvishes,* for I thought that they were not conscious of spirituality. Once I became intimately familiar with what true spirituality was and understood the state those *darvishes* were in, I instead preferred to keep company with the Islamic scholars, for they have truly experienced suffering. These *darvishes* lie when they claim to be genuine ascetics. Where is their asceticism? (Movahed 2012, 249)

It seems, in fact, that this to and fro between jurisprudence and spirituality continued throughout Shams's life and often created confusion for those who did not know him. They could not comprehend or discern how his adherence to Islamic laws, which was paramount to his existence, could be paired with his total devotion to Sufism. He recounts:

> They asked a friend of mine about me: "Is he a theologian or a *darvish?*" He replied: "He's both." They asked: "Then why does he always talk about

jurisprudence?" He answered: "Because spirituality is not a subject that he could speak about with this group! He speaks in terms of the law because he's hiding his meaning and revealing secrets in between the lines." (Movahed 1997, 58)

The Sufi path is a narrow one, slippery and full of fast, sharp turns. If one slips off, on one side lies the rugged terrain of zeal for asceticism, the obsession with denying oneself any pleasure and belittling one's body, and on the other side lies the cesspool of corruption, laziness, and uselessness. In the thirteenth century, the Persians were not only religious but extremely traditional, more so than the neighboring Turks, Syrians, and Mesopotamians and the more distant Egyptians, but still, corruption and the desire to climb socially was rife among many Islamic theologians and scholars.

Shams and most pure-hearted Sufis must have been painfully aware of this situation in their native Azarbaijân, and they suffered as they watched their colleagues engage in self-motivated aggrandizement. In his *Maghâlât,* Shams repeatedly criticizes these hypocrites and reproaches them for misleading the young who sought their guidance: "These men who speak from the pulpits and lead the prayers are the thieves of our religion!" (Movahed 2009, 212).

"TRAVEL" AS A MEANS
OF EDUCATION

In the Sufi tradition of master and pupil, or shaykh/*pīr*/ *morshed* and *morīd,* at one point after having served one's mentor for some years and having completed the necessary preliminary stages of *solûk,* or Sufi training, a student was sent away on a trip. Often, these trips happened without prior planning but could occur as a result of the *morīd* experiencing overexcitement or excessive periods of ecstasy.

Separation from one's mentor was intended to mature the devotee and was never allowed until one's shaykh was convinced of the need for it. To be apart from one's mentor was supposed to increase the *morīd*'s love for him, meanwhile maturing the *morīd* out of necessity and teaching him how to stand on his own two feet, as he would no longer enjoy the protection he had been offered previously by his shaykh. Shams perhaps recollects his own experience when he tells a *morīd*:

> I worry for you at this hour because, unaware of the
> hardships of separation, you are happily sleeping
> in the cool shadow of your shaykh's compassion.
> With one wrong move you can lose this mercy and
> afterward can only dream of regaining it; neither

will you ever be able to see your shaykh again without his will, whether in your sleep or while you're awake. Hope is valuable and wise when the possibility of achieving is real, otherwise what's the use? (Movahed 2009, 67)

The concept of travel was indeed meant to symbolize inner travel and the constant inner search for the divine and perfection. Shams admits: "When the *morīd* is not yet perfected, it is not wise for him to be separated from his shaykh. But when he becomes a perfect Sufi, his mentor's absence will cause him no harm" (Movahed 2012, 144–45).

The importance of being separated from one's revered *morshed* or shaykh becomes apparent in Shams's relationship with Rumi many years later, when Shams tells Rumi that he himself will tolerate the hardship of travel for Rumi's sake, because he can't expect Rumi, who had many social and family responsibilities, to just pick up and leave town:

Were you able to do something such that I didn't have to go away for your benefit and we could attain what is necessary without the need for travel, it would indeed be worthwhile, for I am unable to order you to go away. I shall, therefore, take it upon myself to endure the trouble of traveling, because separation matures one. While separated from each other, one begins to think about all the things that one should have said openly, and how easy it would have been to be straightforward instead of saying everything in puzzles in an effort to avoid discord. It would have been so much easier than tolerating the hardships of travel and being separated. If need be I will take fifty trips for your sake, for what does it matter to me if I go away or not! It is all for your improvement; otherwise, what difference does it make if I were in Rûm or in Damascus, in Mecca or in Istanbul? It makes no difference to me, other than certainly traveling matures the person in many ways. (Movahed 2009, 74–75)

These extensive travels during which Sufis would forsake their homes and family were frowned upon by classical Islamic leaders and deemed disagreeable by Sharia law. However, the Sufi masters considered this forsaking of one's home and life in general necessary for the education of their students, whereby, having given up on everything familiar, they would instead turn to God. Becoming acquainted with unknown horizons, alone and downtrodden, often in the dark of night, they would experience incredibly deep and meaningful visions and gain spiritual acumen. Thus travel, regarded as character building, often became an essential part of Sufi education, during which the *morīd* would "cook" while separated from his beloved master who had spiritually looked after him until then.

THE SEARCH FOR THE
PERFECT SHAYKH

In Tabriz, the great spiritual masters in Shams's time were mostly what he calls *ommi,* meaning that they were not necessarily educated and had received their spiritual wisdom directly from spiritual sources rather than by studying books and attending school. They were *majzoub,* mad in the love of God, enchanted almost, and a few were susceptible to falling into unusual states of consciousness and behaving rather rashly. Their knowledge was innate, and even if some were illiterate, they had more inherent wisdom than most educated shaykhs. Shams must have been familiar with and perhaps even close to many of them. Nevertheless, when he was about twenty years old, he chose to leave Tabriz in search of a higher *pīr* or perhaps was sent away by Shaykh Seleh-Bâf after having completed his initial Sufi training (Movahed 1997, 83).

Years later, he confessed to Rumi that Seleh-Bâf had taught him many things but had not realized the gem that lay in Shams's being, which Rumi did. In fact, Shams eventually found the perfect shaykh in himself, and he was able to transfer that perfection to Rumi when they were finally united. The essential "need" of a person to find truth in life had become paraamount to Shams's existence, and although he was still so young, he was nevertheless well aware that he needed the help of a higher master to guide him through. He says:

> The world is not without a perfect shaykh, and I left my hometown in search of such a man. However, I found no such shaykh, not even one who could remain indifferent to people's gossip, which is the first step on the hundred-thousand-year journey to perfection. In the end, though, I found Mowlânâ, who embodied perfection, and that's precisely why I chose to sit in conversation with him and decided to move from Aleppo to Konya. (Movahed 1997, 65)

After he left Tabriz, Shams traveled extensively, earning himself the title "Flying Shams." A few places that he's known to have visited and stayed in are Baghdad, Damascus, Aleppo, Kayseri, Aksaray, Sivas, Erzerum, and Erzincan (Movahed 1997, 67). Shams refused to stay in *kâneghâhs,* where his room and board would have been free, preferring to stay in paying caravanserais and earning his keep by teaching young pupils. This didn't earn him much but was a respectable profession. In fact, Shams had developed a method by which he was able to teach the entire Koran to a young pupil in only three months. Teaching, however, required long stays in one place, and Shams had managed to do so in Damascus and Aleppo, but when he chose not to stay long in other cities, he had to earn his living in another fashion.

While as a young man he often did manual labor until late into the night despite his general frailty, he's known to have woven girdles for trousers in his later years. He confesses that he had gone to Erzincân to find work as a builder, but because of his weak constitution, no one would employ him. During his stays in various towns, he experienced many difficulties, as he was too honest and, as a straight talker, refused to praise those he deemed to be unworthy. He was considered too poor and weak to be respected, and often he was literally thrown out of town.

On many occasions when he found himself penniless, he would seek shelter for the night in mosques, and much to his dismay would find that the house of God was not truly the domain of the Almighty but had a human caretaker who needed to be satisfied monetarily; thus, he would be turned away even from mosques. Often, purely because of his Turkish accent when he spoke Arabic, being from Tabriz, people would belittle him and call him a crazy ass! (Sâheb-Zamâni 1990, 83–84).

Tolerating the injustice leveled against him by unintelligent folk and experiencing complete and utter poverty and homelessness at times, Shams nevertheless continued to revere life and refused to see anything other than beauty in the world, albeit remaining cautious about revealing his true self to people he deemed incapable of understanding him. He said, "When I am joyful, even if the whole world were seeped in sorrow it would not affect me, and if I were sad I would never allow anyone to get affected by me either!" (Movahed 2009, 143).

FORMATIVE YEARS

Shams felt an unbending brotherhood with the down-trodden and the poor, those who had been shunned by society and cast aside by the wealthy; he considered himself their forbearer. He watched the injustice, the demise of principles and morality in all echelons of society, and privately suffered from being a witness to the unnecessary misery of the masses. He openly questioned the misplacement of empathy and love, while pointing his finger at the culprits.

In Shams's world, one cried for the living not for the dead. While he was unwilling to serve as a guide for unintelligent, common people, Shams considered himself responsible for pointing out the truth to their shaykhs, while he searched for the "perfect man" from among them (Sâheb-Zamâni 1990, 389). Shams did not in fact use the term "perfect man" but rather used different terms such as perfect shaykh, perfect ones, perfect and imperfect ones, special ones, perfection, or God's special one—all of which refer to the ultimate maturity of man, worthy of admiration, praise, and respect (Sâheb-Zamâni 1990, 580–81).

Even acknowledging the rarity of the perfect man, Shams held that his personality would have to embrace fourteen essential attributes:

1. Wisdom and Reason
2. Inner Vision
3. Consciousness of the Times
4. Consciousness of the Self
5. Self-Control
    a. Spiritual Wealth
    b. Spiritual Balance
    c. Clarity in Discernment
6. Self-Help and Self-Determination
7. Social Consciousness
8. Self-Sacrifice
9. Freedom and Promotion of Independence
10. Humility, yet Combativeness when Faced with Injustice
11. The Exercise of No Judgment
12. Love and Idealism
13. Authenticity and Creativity
14. Perseverance and Stability (Sâheb-Zamâni 1990, 583)

Hiding behind teaching young pupils and remaining mysteriously unknown to peers was a common practice among spiritual masters, and Shams was an expert at it. He also did not hesitate to do manual labor to hide his identity, and he disappeared instantly from any town if he felt that he had been recognized as a high Sufi; perhaps this is another reason why he came to be known as "Flying Shams."

In one episode related by Fereydoun Sepahsâlâr, one of Rumi's main biographers, during his stay in Damascus, Shams would buy the minimum possible amount of mutton stew from a shop, soak only dry bread in it, and live on that for a whole week. After a while, the shop owner realized that Shams was in fact intentionally adhering to a fast and that he must be a high-standing *darvish*. The next time Shams went to purchase his weekly share of the stew, the owner made sure to give him an ample amount and added two fresh loaves of bread to his order. Shams realized that his cover had been blown, and the next day he left town (Sâheb-Zamâni 1990, 29).

Unlike Shams, there were many Sufi shaykhs who did not hide their identity and who lived gainful lives in their societies. A few of Shams's contemporaries who earned their living by having regular jobs instead of freeloading off their *morîds* were Shaykh Seleh-Bâf, who wove baskets; Ajbâdi, who had a silk-weaving workshop; and Attâr, who had a pharmacy. Sufis often had titles reflecting their professions, such as grocer, haberdasher, saddlebag maker, potter, gardener, fishmonger, glassmaker, ironmonger, calligrapher, teacher, etc.

Rising from among the masses, these Sufi masters attracted common people because they spoke to them in a language they understood, the everyday language of the streets. Not only were they honest and approachable, but they were also the people's own, speaking kindly to their charges without boasting of their own knowledge. They managed their Sufism by bringing prayer and faith together with music and *samâ,* which greatly appealed to the general masses who sought relief from the dictatorial behavior of their rulers.

If Shams had left Tabriz at about twenty years of age and had arrived in Konya to meet with Rumi at the ripe age of sixty, then he must have spent the forty interim years traveling from place to place, but we cannot be certain of the number of years he might have spent in any one specific town. It was during these travels that he met many great men of his age and spent time with them in their gatherings and classes. Shahâb Heriveh (or Heravi) in Damascus, whom Shams sometimes called "Khorâssani," was one of them:

> Shahab never accepted anyone into his private gatherings. He would say, "Gabriel is a burden for me, even I am a burden to me!" Yet despite his distaste for company he would tell me, "You can come because you bring peace to my heart." (Movahed 1997, 85)

Other renowned Iranian contemporaries of Shams include Khajeh Abdollah Ansâri, Abol Hassan Kharaghâni, Bayazid Bastâmi, and Baba Taher Oriyân. Highly regarded by Shams, the renowned Fakhr-e Râzi, a contemporary of Shahâbeddin Yahyâ Sohrevardi, with whom he shared the same teacher, Majd-e Gilâni, was a successful philosopher who was popular with the rulers of the time. Basking in his pride, however, Fakhr-e Râzi did not respect many of his contemporaries, which brought him ample jealousy and dislike. Much to his admirers' discontent, he refuted all of his research and writings in his last will and testament shortly before his death, rendering them worthless.

Shams was a keen admirer of Sohrevardi, or Shaykh-e Eshrâgh, as well; he had penned *Hekmat-ol Eshrâgh,* a thesis on Eastern and specifically Iranian Sufi masters and their thinking. Sohrevardi was strangled for heresy at the age of thirty-six, having already written over fifty philosophical theses and books. Shams also venerated Shaykh Mohammad, also known as Mohiyeddin Mohammad or Shaykh Akbar but better known in the West as Ibn Arabi, who must have been twenty years his senior and was close to Shams of Khuy, whose private classes Shams attended in Damascus. Shams eventually gave up on Shams of Khuy, rather smugly stating:

I left the juror Shams al-Din because he could no longer teach me. He said to me, "I cannot be ashamed before God; He has created you perfectly, and I see a precious gem and am unable to add to its beauty." (Movahed 2012, 221)

Ibn Arabi was one of the most respected Sufi masters of the day and was considered an exceptional character whose greatness was unrivaled by his contemporaries. Shams amiably referred to him as a most "kind sympathizer" and "excellent companion," and above all "a mountain, a great mountain." Ibn Arabi, who was also well acquainted with Shahâb Heravi and had dreamed about the latter's death, was quite fond of Shams and used to call him "son" or "brother" (Movahed 1997, 101).

Yet when Shams met Rumi years later, he admitted: "Shaykh Mohammad [Ibn Arabi] prayed constantly and claimed to be a follower of the Prophet. I learned a great deal from him but nothing like what I've learned from you, Mowlânâ! It's like comparing pebbles with pearls!" (Movahed 2009, 144).

Ohad al-Din Kermâni was another *pīr* and a contemporary of Shams, albeit much older, and he was eager to recruit Shams into his circle. But Shams suspected him of being too keen on young, handsome *morīds,* a tendency that he abhorred. Shams related:

This shaykh took me with him to the *samâ* cere-
mony and paid me much respect, and he invited
me into his private sessions. He asked me one day:
"What if you came and spent time with me for
a while?" I told him: "I will if you agree to bring
two cups of wine, one for me and one for you, and
when the *samâ* begins we will take turns drinking."
He said, "I cannot!" I told him: "Then my company
and conversation is not for you. You should be
prepared to give up your *morīds* and the rest of
the world for this one cup of wine!" (Movahed
1997, 95)

This was indeed an impossible task for the respectable elderly shaykh, but Shams knew what he was doing.
He wanted to cut off all hope for the shaykh to engage
him, and therefore he presented him with this unattain-
able challenge. He also wished to demonstrate his own
state of being *lâubâlî*, or carefree, not only showing the
minimum amount of respect for superficial social norms
but also going to extensive lengths to exaggerate his dislike and disregard for them.

Shams refers to Ohad al-Din in his *Maghâlât* when
he discusses the four stages of "spiritual drunkenness,"
or spiritual growth, proposing that the shaykh and his
morīds were stuck primarily in the realm of "drunkenness

on air," the first of the four stages. Being "drunk on air" does not necessarily mean to be drunk on the world of gold, women, and materialism in general but rather to be in an unsettled or disheveled state marked by a loss of self, a state often experienced by younger monks and yogis and those who have forsaken the material world and its physical pleasures.

Once, when Shams saw Ohad al-Din staring into a basin, he asked him what he was doing, and the shaykh responded: "I'm watching the moon's reflection in the water." Shams retorted, "If you don't have a stiff neck, why don't you look directly at the moon instead? You need to find a physician to cure you!" (Movahed 1997, 96).

SPIRITUAL MATURITY

It is obvious that Shams did not consider Ohad al-Din to be among the "perfect men" he was seeking, and he named the first stage of spiritual growth the "Ohad-aneh" stage, alluding to and belittling Ohad al-Din's immature young spirituality. The four stages of "spiritual drunkenness," according to Shams, are:

1. Drunk on the World of Air—alluding to the state of imagination, with a high chance of going astray.
2. Drunk on the World of Spirit—alluding to the state of knowledge.
3. Drunk on God's Path—alluding to the state of imagination, without the chance of going astray.
4. Drunk on God—alluding to the opening of the eyes.

The first stage of "Air" is the domain of "Imagination," where the potential to make mistakes is enormous. Next is the stage of "Knowledge," which offers a certain degree of spiritual certainty followed by another state of "Imagination," which does not offer the potential for mistakes, and finally comes the state of "Opening of Eyes."

When Shams speaks of "Imagination," he's referring to an inner strength and innate power that guides one's life that is not yet fully mature, much like that of a child, prone to stumbling and injury. In the "Knowledge" stage, the child still requires a caring nanny to look after him and help him stand on his own feet, teaching him to distinguish between right and wrong, until he reaches maturity or the stage of "Opening of Eyes," alluding to the development of full insight and the attainment of perfection (Movahed 1997, 96).

The two foremost concepts that Shams advises adhering to in the mystic path are "spiritual drunkenness" and "following the prophet." Submitting to and being a disciple of the Prophet as well as one's *pīr* is one of the pillars of Islam as well as Sufism. Such was Shams's devotion to the Prophet that he admitted: "I don't bow to the Koran because it is God's words but because the Prophet Mohammad has uttered them!" (Movahed 1997, 117).

Shams was acutely aware of the possibility of falling into false traps when initially becoming acquainted with Sufism, of confusing such traps with the glory of the real path, symbolized by the Prophet. He warned of the dangers of imitation, always lurking in the background, that can turn one's desire for mysticism into a cult of personality, mistaking the initial state of "drunkenness" for the ultimate spiritual state:

> Every instance of dishonesty and corruption in the world has resulted from someone imitating someone else, either copying them or refuting them. Imitation causes a person to blow hot and cold, as he

encounters something different every day. If on one occasion he were to come across the truth and wish to change his mind about a matter he had equivocated about earlier, he must hide it, for people will know that he has been imitating others until then. He won't reveal anything, because he risks losing people's trust as well as all self-confidence in himself. (Movahed 2009, 73)

Spiritual drunkenness is a state of selflessness in which a spiritual warrior naturally adopts fatalism. Each of the four stages of Shams's spirituality embodies some degree of drunkenness accompanied by fatalism; yet he considers fatalism a weak episode in one's journey, one that must be surmounted to attain the perfect consciousness that lies beyond it. Poets speak of the man slaying wine, while Shams speaks of wine slaying the man: "The more he drinks, the more conscious he becomes; he drinks to the limit and still becomes more conscious, provoking the entire world and the universe into complete and utter consciousness!" (Movahed 1997, 119). He insists that people drink wine to become drunk, but he belongs to the realm of "Love" and is drunk all the time!

For Shams, the perfect model of this consciousness was the Prophet Mohammad, and he believed that following the Prophet would lead one to a state of perfection or consciousness beyond drunkenness. This devotion had to be consummate for one to attain the object of one's desire, where the light that shone in the Prophet's eyes could finally be discerned. In this state there is no longer "I" or "me," for one has dissolved into the Truth. Hope was the only consolation, and the heart that contained hope was indeed the nest of "Union."

Shams's way differed from that of other Sufis, who easily became lost in their first esoteric experiences, either feigning selflessness or actually believing themselves to have touched it, screaming and shouting uncontrollably in their delusion. Shams considered the Prophet's coming into the faith at the age of forty a sign of his maturity, as opposed to Jesus of Nazareth's alleged wisdom and self-knowledge at a very young age. Shams followed the Prophet, and the Prophet did not perform forty-day retreats or refrain from leading a normal life. Likewise, Shams insisted that one should not avoid living among normal people but that one should conduct one's life such that one doesn't become one *with* the crowd but only one *among* them.

> An ascetic who lives in a cave is a mountain man and no longer a human, for if he were, he'd be living among men who are intelligent and worthy of God's wisdom. What business do men have living in a cave? If man were made of mud then he would

be attracted to rocks, but what can a man want with rocks? Do not go into *khalvat* or seclusion and solitude; remain an individual in the midst of a crowd, but be alone and remember that the Prophet says: "In Islam there is no monasticism." (Movahed 2009, 214)

Although Shams proposed that one should not give up on living among people, as far as we know, he successfully hid his true self all his life, except when he was in Konya with Rumi. Although self-sufficient, in emotional terms he remained angry, unsatisfied, inward looking, and unsettled, even when he was in Rumi's company (Sâheb-Zamâni 1990, 162).

Shams was an impatient man who did not seek an audience; he did not look for "customers" and had no need to trick the public. His method was the opposite of the norm; he believed that the prey should seek the hunter rather than the other way around. He chose his own public and did not waste his time simplifying his speech so that it would be comprehensible to an inferior level of intelligence; his words were fit only for shaykhs and high-level Sufi ears (Sâheb-Zamâni 1990, 124).

He was a realistic man, though, and did not adhere to inflexible principles of right and wrong. For him, committing a sin and performing a beneficial act were relative behaviors in life and had to be viewed in their different contexts: "Each person commits a transgression only worthy of himself; for one person it's to be a rogue and commit debauchery, while for another it's to be absent before God!" (Movahed 2009, 107).

Contrary to the general concept that the world contains aspects that are either strictly good or strictly evil, Shams believed that it depended on man's own criteria, as we are ultimately responsible for determining our own values and choosing what is evil and detrimental, or beautiful and valuable. Man, therefore, is responsible not only for setting standards and values in the world but also for destroying them; thus, what could be harâm or unacceptable in one instance could be completely halâl or acceptable in another (Sâheb-Zamâni 1990, 149).

SOCIO-HISTORICAL
ATMOSPHERE OF RÛM

The mid-13th century was a time of migration and displacement, as Mongol invasions were devastating the entire region that we know today as the Middle East. Konya, the capital of the Seljuk Sultanate in the region then known as Rûm in central Anatolia, was a multiethnic, multireligious center where boundaries were often crossed. The inhabitants of Konya included Persians, Turks, Greeks, Arabs, Kurds, Armenians, and Jews, among others, from various social classes, some highly educated and some totally illiterate (Pifer 2014, 29, 32).

It was during this time that regional rulers in Rûm encouraged charismatic Sufi masters to emigrate there and cultivate their own religious and cultural heritage, but also to help integrate the heterogeneous influx of immigrants into local society in the aftermath of the Mongol invasion. The invitation of Rumi's father, Baha'eddin Valad or Sultan ol-Ulama ("Master of All Scholars"), from Khorāsān by the Seljuk leaders in the midst of this regional upheaval and the establishment of a school for him in Konya to preach and organize a following are examples of this policy (Pifer 2014, 32, 33).

In fact, Rumi's father had had a similar offer from the grandees of Damascus, but he had refused it because he deemed the atmosphere of that city to be morally and socially corrupt, and he found it impossible to tolerate the pervasive repression by the city's rulers. He had reluctantly sought to leave his hometown of Balkh, in today's Afghanistan, with his family and followers because of the cruelty of Khârazm Shah, and he wasn't about to succumb to some other merciless and vindictive ruler.

Shams's era was indeed a time of war, famine, earthquakes, cholera, and destructive power mongering between the nations of the region. At a time when money ruled, and people were poor and hungry, deluded by their rulers and terrorized by invading Mongols, it was not a surprise that they had lost their faith in their protectors and their justice system and found themselves attracted to Sufis and their promise of spirituality (Sâheb-Zamâni 1990, 231–36). In Sufism, they hoped to reach the golden promise of eternal love, which they trusted would clear their hearts of anger, prejudice, and hate, creating peace and security and thus illuminating the path of life here and hereafter.

SHAMS IN KONYA

When Shams first arrived in Konya in October 1244, he had been searching for a companion to share his insight and wisdom since leaving his native Tabriz forty years earlier. We notice that in the *Maghâlât,* he says that he had begged God to let him find and mix with wise men with whom he could engage intellectually. For Shams, Sufism was a religion of love, and he needed intelligent conversations with men who knew what spiritual love entailed: "I needed someone of my own caliber so I could make a Mecca of him and turn to him, for I had become weary of myself" (Movahed 2009, 98).

He had a dream in which he was told that he would meet with a *valī,* or representative of God on earth, in Rûm, but that he would have to wait, as it was still not the right time. At least fifteen or sixteen years before their final union in Konya, Shams had in fact met Rumi, probably in Damascus, and had even spoken to him: "My heart was settled on you from the very beginning, but I could tell from our conversation that you were not yet ready to hear my secrets. You were not in the right state of mind then, but now is the hour!" (Movahed 2009, 170).

He confessed to Rumi when they reunited: "The purpose of creation is for two friends to meet and sit before each other, to encounter God away from all temptations. The purpose of creation is not bread or the baker, meat or the butcher; it is all about this instance when I am in the company of Mowlânâ!" (Movahed 2009, 174). For Shams, "Love" was the reflection of God's beauty. He believed that everything that God had created stemmed from the essence of his own unrivalled beauty, and one could only begin to fathom spiritual "Love" when one caught a glimpse of that original and eternal beauty.

At the time of Shams, the streets of Konya must have been adorned with an array of various ethnic backgrounds, each garbed in their own specific style of colorful clothing and headdress. The unpaved back alleys were so narrow that two people could hardly pass without brushing against each other. The merchants' quarters, where people did their daily shopping, were also the hub of much social activity. As was his custom, when Shams arrived in Konya, he took up residence in a caravanserai in the rice merchants' quarters, according to one source (Fereydoun Sepahsâlâr), or in the sugar merchants' quarters, according to another (Ahmed Aflâki).

As there is a gap of 120 years between these two scholars, we can probably assume that the rice quarters had changed to sugar quarters during the interim. Today, nothing remains of this district, but then it was an area of small stalls and booths, where learned men and intellectuals would meet and converse.

About a month after he arrived in Konya, Shams was sitting in one of these booths when Rumi arrived, allegedly on horseback, and with his entourage took a seat across from Shams. In the past, this spot was referred to as the Marj al-Bahrayn, or the meeting place of two seas, adopted from a Koranic verse in the sura of al-Rahmân. *Marj* means to mix using outside effort or to remove boundaries so that two things can naturally mix together. In the Koran, this verse refers to the mixing of two seas, one salty and the other sweet, left to themselves so they can mingle yet retain their own integrity and specific characteristics, including their own color and taste (Movahed 1997, 108).

Shams says in the *Maghâlât,* which is the most reliable source for this meeting, that he posed a question to Rumi referring to Bâyazid Bastâmi, the Iranian Sufi master. He asked Rumi: "Why did Bâyazid say, 'Glory to me, how great is my majesty' and not 'We do not know Thee as it is befitting,' like the Prophet used to say when he prayed to God?"

Bâyazid believed that he had found God and considered himself complete, and he looked no further to improve his spiritual state. The Prophet, however, after he had already achieved spiritual perfection, continued until his last hour to look further, seeking to encounter God's grandeur with greater and greater intensity, and still he said that he did not perceive God as befitted him.

Rumi, who was a genuine perfectionist, immediately understood what Shams was referring to and where this question was leading. Shams says that at that point, Rumi became "drunk" on the meaning of those words, and their unique friendship began. They shunned the company of everyone else and sat in *khalvat,* or in private, for three months initially, avoiding all interruption by Rumi's students and followers (Sâheb-Zamâni 1990, 20).

THE *MAGHÂLÂT* OR
DISCOURSES OF SHAMS

Until the *Maghâlât* of Shams was discovered and collected as a whole in 1970—first by Ahmad Khowshnevis,
followed by Nasseredin Sâheb-Zamâni in *The Third
Script* in 1972, and finally by Mohammad Ali Movahed in the final edition of the *Maghâlât* in 1977 (Lewis
2000, 136)—it was literally impossible to make any valid
assumptions about the life and character of Shams. Some
thought that he hadn't even existed, that he was only a
figment of Rumi's imagination.

The original copy of the *Maghâlât* was in Rumi's
possession; he had made notes in the margins, and subsequently the scribe who copied this collection for study
by *morīds* faithfully copied Rumi's notes, marking them
with red ink. Rumi and his followers referred to Shams's
Maghâlât as "Shams's Secrets," and they must have repeatedly referred to them in the years after his disappearance
(Movahed 2008, 360).

The *Maghâlât* is a collection of sayings by Shams
while he was in Konya, including his thoughts, bits of
advice, anecdotes, statements about himself and his state
of mind, feelings about his relationship with Rumi, his
opinions of other Sufis and scholars, and his feelings and
understanding about people in general and a few people

in particular. They show us that Shams spent time not only in Rumi's company but also with other Sufi masters in Konya, and we can determine from the text that Rumi was not always present during these talks.

As mentioned earlier, the *Maghâlât* was not written by Shams but compiled from notes taken by a follower who was present in the closed circle of these intimate conversations. These notes were never edited for publication, and they remained in the form of haphazard musings until the 20th century. Some parts, however, do read smoothly, and it's believed that they must have been dictated by Shams himself. Nevertheless, the *Maghâlât* comes across mainly as a body of disconnected talks, presented in plain colloquial language, often hindered by faulty grammar in which the subjects are sometimes obscure and the context elusive.

The fact that Shams frequently spoke in parables alluding to issues, and that he tended to hop from one subject to another without concluding any of them, makes comprehension difficult. It is not known for sure whether the apparent disparity of the text is due to the scribe's slow hand or to Shams's haphazard presentation; we are not even sure if the conversations were held in sequence as they appear in the *Maghâlât* or occurred arbitrarily or whether they took place over minutes, hours, or days.

Dr. Movahed's abridged version of the *Maghâlât*, called *Khomi az Sharâb-e Rabani* (*A Cup of Divine Wine*), in which he clarifies many questions simply by using punctuation (which was unknown in the old Persian writing tradition), renders the work much easier to understand and thus to admire, despite the structural difficulties of the text.

Shams uses many poems to demonstrate his points, but none of them are his own, and most are not exceptional representatives of the best Persian verse. When he chose to speak, his words were often cloaked in humor that concealed his meaning; he confessed to this tactic, stating that his audience was incapable of digesting his unadulterated speech. Other times, he was intentionally sarcastic to stress a certain point. His humor was aimed not at his audience as individuals but at the general lack of substance, the absence of principles, and the destructiveness of prejudice among men; his targets were faulty ideals and causes, not individual people.

Shams was an inward-looking man, full of secrets and comfortable with his inner life, having chosen to protect himself from the masses by "concealing himself" and "testing people," the two principles by which he operated his life (Sâheb-Zamâni 1990, 134–35). His demeanor, by which he considered himself apart from and superior to people in general, together with his unrelenting self-confidence, short temper, and pride, did not warm him to many and distanced him from people's hearts. The tumultuous times he lived in undoubtedly contributed to his habit of concealing his true self, and he confesses: "Sometimes there's no other way but to keep silent and to surrender!" (Movahed 2009, 59).

Movahed believes that, from Shams's tone of voice, he must have been familiar with Rumi's father (Baha'eddin Valad) and his companions, especially Seyyed Borhânne-din Mohaghegh, who looked after Rumi throughout his initial Sufi training and after the death of his father. Shams must have met them while they were in Damascus and attended their gatherings but had not made himself known to them. Such stealth would have been easy for Shams, as he did not adopt the Sufi garb or stay in *khânegâhs* or madrasas, and he did menial jobs to earn his keep.

We understand from the *Maghâlât* that when Shams arrived in Konya at the age of sixty, he was a gaunt man with a thin beard who appeared weak but in fact was extremely quick and nimble, with great stamina and warm, penetrating speech; a man who was completely self-confident and in control of himself. He had total belief in his own ideas and principles and was absolutely intolerant of superficial customs and formalities. He

A LITTLE BOOK OF MYSTICAL SECRETS

came across as ambitious and lofty but extremely private, reserved, and inward looking, yet he was highly excitable, cutting, and quarrelsome. He could remain silent for hours on end, listening to others, but once he began to speak, he did not tolerate any interference or criticism. He respected the common sciences but found them useless in the search for truth.

Shams wanted nothing to do with the Sufi customs of cutting the hair, engaging in initiations, teaching the *zekr* (the ninety-nine names of God), or sending novices on forty-day retreats; but he strongly believed in the importance of having a *pīr* as a guide on the path of spiritual growth. He was tolerant and patient with strangers but expected nothing less than total submission from friends. His manner of teaching, on which he firmly insisted, was to ask for more than anyone could possibly offer; he thus harbored unrealistically high expectations of his friends and sometimes hurt their feelings.

He said: "I have nothing to do with the masses, it's not for them that I've come. I have come for the sake of those who guide people to God. I've come to put my finger on *their* jugular vein!" (Movahed 2009, 32).

And elsewhere he reiterates:

Until they learn to trust me unconditionally and respect me in public, I shall be harsh with friends. They ask why am I kind to strangers and unkind to them? I simply ask them, how can they not see my undying kindness toward them? I also tell them that if the great saints in all their glory were alive and could see us together, their highest wish would be to sit with us for a moment! I aim my harshness at those I love most, but it's in order for them to give up their antagonism and distrust so that I can make them privy to my secrets, for these traits should not exist in God's creations. (Movahed 2009, 58)

Despite his insistence on keeping his privacy, when Shams took residence in Konya, he nevertheless gained a reputation as a high Sufi, and many people, including the rich, wanted to meet him and learn from him. Being *lâobâlî*, Shams set a very expensive fee for meetings with them. Without caring what his audience thought of the fees, he duly collected them and, unbeknown to his audience, redistributed them among the needy. Shams insisted on considering everyone, including prostitutes, equal in human terms, and in fact he would visit brothels, where he would donate the money he had received from the rich.

> Let's go to the whorehouse to pay a visit to those poor souls, hasn't God created them too? Never mind if they are sinful or not, let's go and see them anyway; let's go to the church as well and see the people there too. Not many can tolerate my work, what I do is not for hypocrites! (Movahed 2009, 143)

One of Shams's most serious dislikes, however, was not the wealthy but those of all classes who sought and abused young boys, which was a known and popular custom among many. As related above, Shaykh Ohad al-Din was one such Sufi whose admiration for handsome youth repulsed Shams, who quickly and cleverly disengaged himself from the shaykh's company.

He also strictly opposed the use of hashish, which was popular among many *darvishes,* considering it to be the seduction of the devil. When Rumi presented Shams with his son, Sultan Valad, and Shams agreed to be his shaykh, the two things that Shams absolutely prohibited were smoking hashish and indulging in homosexual activity (Saheb-Zamani 1990, 92).

After Rumi and Shams retreated from public life, Shams began to control Rumi's followers' visits. As he did with the rich who wished to meet with him, Shams began to ask Rumi's followers to pay dearly if they wanted to see their master, which offended them greatly. Being faced for the first time with having to pay to see their shaykh, they openly accused Shams of greediness and charlatanry: "Mowlana is free from the world but Shams is not. Mowlana tells us that because we don't like Shams, we accuse him of pettiness, for if we did like him we wouldn't consider it greedy and unlawful of him to ask us to give up our money!" (Movahed 2009, 41).

Shams believed that to part with one's money was the first step on the path of spirituality, and that was the reason why he would press Rumi's followers to pay up. These followers didn't understand Shams's motive, and his requests for payment just added to their dislike of the man who had already stolen their revered master. To them, Shams would say:

> You have many obstacles in your way! Money for most is their Mecca, but the great masters have done away with its claws, and it no longer holds a grip on them. On the other hand, for those who are in love with the world, money is more precious than their sweet life, as if they were not even alive—because if they were, how could money be dearer? (Movahed 2009, 54)

He must have suffered silently as Rumi's students continued their verbal abuse, but he would not give up his way of doing things, as he thought that a friend was like a rose, made of both petals and thorns.

> Many great men lost their affection for me because they thought I was after their money. I wasn't, I was after getting those idiots to *part* with their money! They were great shaykhs and dignitaries, and what could I possibly want with shaykhs and so-called great men? I want *you* the way you are! I want *need*, I want *hunger*, and I want *thirst!* Clear water seeks the thirsty because it is generous and kind. (Movahed 2009, 133)

Although Shams had paramount respect for Rumi, he knew that to convince this highly educated mufti to listen to him, he had to empty him of his learned knowledge to prepare him for further Sufi "burning" or "cooking," a task that required time. There are many sensationalized stories about Rumi and Shams and what may have occurred between these two great men, none of which we can be certain. Yet it may be useful to mention a couple of these dramatized stories that allude to the notion that Shams could perform magical acts.

On one occasion, Shams allegedly walks into Rumi's home and finds him surrounded by his favorite valuable books. Shams asks Rumi: "What are these?" Rumi brushes him aside: "You don't understand about these things." Before Rumi can continue, Shams sets the books on fire; Rumi screams: "What is *this?*" To which Shams responds: "This, *you* don't understand!" Subsequently, Shams returns the books to Rumi untarnished.

In another version of the story, Shams walks into Rumi's house and sees Rumi sitting by the pool with his precious books laid out before him. Shams asks: "What are these?" Rumi replies: "These are just noise and clamor to you, what business could you possibly have with them?" Shams picks up the books and throws them into the pool. "Oh *darvish,* what have you done? Some of these were my beloved father's books, and they can never be replaced!" exclaims Rumi. Shams picks up the books one by one and hands them back to Rumi, unscathed. Rumi asks him in amazement: "What is the secret of this?" To which Shams sniggers: "This is genius! What would you know of *this?*" (Forouzanfar 2006, 97–98).

Many Sufi masters insisted that new pupils throw away their books and put aside everything they had learned until then before entering the Sufi path. Likewise, Shams insisted on a similar method of teaching, whereby he demanded that Rumi give up not only his valuable religious and philosophical manuscripts but even his father's prized book, which was a source of pride and glory for him. Shams insisted on total concentration on the master teacher, complete surrender to his will, and full avoidance of "others." He says:

> The sign of the one who has found his way to me is that others' conversations will seem cold and bitter to him; not that they become uninteresting and he will still continue to talk with them, but that he will never be able to speak with them again! (Movahed 2009, 29–30)

It was indeed Shams's conversation that prompted Rumi to fall in love with him spiritually. Shams asked Rumi to speak with him so that he, in turn, could warm up and begin to speak himself. In fact, from the moment they met and subsequently went into seclusion together, we cannot really be certain of what went on between the two great men other than that from that hour on, Rumi was changed forever.

Shams told Rumi that if he desired Shams to open his heart to him, he had to offer Shams his solitude. Shams believed that not everyone could fall in love but only the heart that had been set on fire was able to rest alone in the silence of love. Shams taught Rumi how to perform the *samâ* for the first time and how to use it as a tool for connecting with God, as he believed that whatever one strived for in one's heart would increase manifold during *samâ:*

> While men turn in *samâ,* God manifests and reveals Himself more clearly to them. They may succeed in going beyond the world they know, but God elevates them beyond other worlds yet unknown and connects them directly with the divine. (Movahed 2009, 29)

Shams criticized Rumi, though, from time to time with regard to what he had learned in books, and he belittled Rumi's relationship with his followers, some of whom were uneducated old criminals and homeless beggars. At the same time, Shams was a great believer in profound friendships and warned people against turning their backs on old and deep friends or becoming too complacent and losing them.

Shams had a jovial and lively approach to life in general, believing in the greatness of man, and he assumed the responsibility of bringing happiness and joy to people around him. He had set himself up as a social messenger, with the aim of completing the incomplete, confirming the perfect ones, supporting the poor, exposing the deceitful, and opposing the oppressors (Sâheb-Zamâni 1990, 82).

Shams did not like to write down his thoughts, as he didn't believe it was possible to capture their essence in written form. Yet he believed that his words would reach those they were meant for once he chose to reveal their meaning, "even after a thousand years!" He insisted that only those who had a "need" in their hearts would understand his meaning, much like Rumi, whose real "need" was for Shams, just as Shams's unflinching "need" was for Rumi:

> Your true self is the one who shows his need! The one who pretended to be needless and a stranger is your enemy; that's why I was torturing him, because he was not the real you. How could I ever hurt you, when I think that if I try to lay a kiss on your feet I am constantly worried that my eyelashes might scratch and blemish your skin? (Movahed 2009, 41)

Shams was on a mission to save Rumi from the "rough companions" who surrounded him. As stated earlier, Shams had met Rumi fifteen or sixteen years before, which he mentions in the *Maghâlât* at least four times, but he had not approached him until he decided it was time. Rumi had to be mentally and spiritually prepared for the appearance of Shams, who had to expose himself to Rumi's senior devotees—who had been among Rumi and his family's *morīd*s and had followed Rumi all the way from Khorasan. These men were now rather seasoned Sufis in their own right and would not look kindly upon a stranger who not only looked like riffraff but was totally unknown to them.

Shams had to be sure that if he were to reveal his wisdom to Rumi and face the wrath of the latter's *morīds,* at least Rumi was spiritually mature enough to fully appreciate him. Rumi was a learned religious leader who walked in his great father's shadow, but he had earned hundreds if not thousands of followers in Konya on his own merit. He was not an empty pot; he was full of knowledge and enjoyed a high social standing. Shams had to empty him of all this knowledge, which he considered only a hindrance, so that he could be prepared for what Shams was about to divulge to him.

Rumi had to give up his "pharaoh-like" pride and learn to hang his head low, because none of his acquired knowledge could help him on the true path to God. Shams thought that if God were hidden behind seven veils of light, then the key to them could only be "Love." Rumi had to be slapped, so that his air of pompousness would be dispelled for good. All that he had already mastered were only so many veils obscuring his vision; now he had to shun everything he had learned before and understand that his path was more than simply being a *pīr* or a *morīd*. Shams believed that human beings were ultimately responsible for themselves, that they must find the "treasure" within and not outside in the cruel world, and he needed Rumi to come to believe this as well.

Shams taught Rumi how to play and enjoy music and how to express his spiritual insights in verse while doing the *samâ,* which Shams considered as necessary as the required five daily prayers (Sâheb-Zamâni 1990, 75). For the first time, Rumi learned that beyond the socially accepted forms of piety such as praying and fasting, going on pilgrimages, practicing Islamic jurisprudence, and controlling one's desires and passions, there was another form of spirituality that embodied the love and joy experienced in becoming acquainted with God.

In the recorded history of Iranian Sufism, Shams was the first to propose that music, dance, poetry, and mysticism should mingle and affect each other equally, thus perfecting one another. To this day, these activities maintain their influence and importance in the school of Rumi, called the Mowlaviyeh School in Iran, and among the Mevlevis in Turkey. According to one source, Rumi continued the *samâ* ceremonies until his last days and held weekly sessions even for women in Konya (Sâheb-Zamâni 1990, 74).

Shams had immediately declared that he had not come to Konya to become Rumi's shaykh, as the person imagining himself capable of taking that position had not yet been born; and he himself could never become anyone's *morīd*. Thus we can only call them companions, each as important as the other for their spiritual advancement. Shams admitted that he was searching for that specific pain that he was unwilling to exchange for a hundred cures; and he wanted to know if Rumi could be that delectable pain.

Although brief, the time that Rumi spent with Shams was the most exhilarating period of Rumi's life. For them, the only purpose for being together and learning from each other was to come closer to God, closer to the absolute Truth. Rumi idolized his friend, for he believed that he had seen the face of God in Shams, and in turn Shams confessed that he had also seen the face of God in Rumi. As Rumi versified:

Shams, Light of God, from Tabriz
in the clear mirror of your being

if I see anything but God
I must be an infidel

From looking at some of the names that Rumi calls Shams in his *Divan-e Shams-e Tabrizi,* we can grasp how highly he revered his beloved companion. Here it might be worth mentioning a few of those names to demonstrate the depth of Rumi's respect and love: Sun of Ultimate Truth, Pride of all Prophets, Divine Manifestation, King of Truth and Meaning, Sultan of the Soul of Sultans, Origin of All Souls, Soul of the Soul of All Souls, Sun of Spirit, Sun of Truth and Faith, Spring of Soul, King of Soul, King of All Religions, King of Kings, King of the King of Spirit, Origin of Faith, Chosen of the Chosen of God's Secret, Symbol of Spirit, Sun of the Times, Infinite Love, Placeless Prophet, Source of the Original Spirit, Pure Light, Gem of Joy, Manifestation of Vision, Absolute Spirit, Flowing Light, Fire of Love of Placelessness, Chinese Painter, Sum of All Being, Master of the Unseen, Sword of Truth, Vision of Truth, Protector of the World of Revelation, Sea of Mercy, Sun of Grace, Lord of the Lord of Mysteries, The Great One, Pure Light . . . and many more.

Their closeness and the fact that Shams was exceptionally strict with Rumi's followers, most of whom he regarded as unworthy of Rumi's company, soon turned most of those followers against Shams. They disliked him intensely and would slander and belittle Shams in public, as he had stolen and estranged their beloved teacher from them. About them, Shams says:

> I prefer the person who curses me to the one who tells my praise, for praising should be expressed in such a manner that there's no denial afterward, which would create conflict. The one who provokes disharmony is indeed worse than the infidel. (Modaress-Sâdeghi 1994, 262)

SHAMS LEAVES KONYA
FOR THE FIRST TIME

After about a year and a half, in March 1246, Shams left Konya for Syria, as he no longer could bear the terrible treatment at the hands of Rumi's students. He might have also decided to take a trip, as he mentions in the *Maghâlât,* for Rumi's benefit, as he didn't feel that he could order Rumi to go away. Nevertheless, a distraught Rumi withdrew from those students, whom he blamed for Shams's mistreatment, and only kept company with *morīds* who had not plotted against his beloved companion.

Meanwhile, Shams spent at least seven months in Syria, where he must have supported himself by doing odd jobs. He wrote at least one letter to Rumi during his absence, which would have confirmed for Rumi that his companion was in fact in Syria. Rumi in turn wrote him many letters imploring him to come back, and Rumi's better-off and guilt-ridden *morīds* donated much gold and silver as travel expenses to convince Shams to return to Konya.

In the end, Rumi sent his eldest son Sultan Valad, who admired Shams and considered him his shaykh, to bring Shams back in October or November 1246 (Lewis 2000, 179). Sultan Valad was successful in his mission, but he refused to ride a horse while in Shams's company out of respect for his *pīr* and chose to walk alongside him during the entire journey from Damascus back to Konya, which took about a month. Being the relentless character that he was, Shams refused to admit that being separated from Rumi had affected him one bit:

> In reality, no one can accompany me, for I am *lâobâlī!* Being separated from Mowlânâ does not bother me, nor does union with him bring me much pleasure, for my joy comes from within me, as does my pain! It's not easy to live with someone like me. (Movahed 2009, 231)

Shams's Sufism is one of action and not just words. One could experiment and fail, but one had to try and try again until gradually one's heart was opened to love, thus freeing one to soar to one's aspired perfection. Shams told Sultan Valad, on seeing him in Damascus:

> Just talking knowledgeably about an issue does not make it possible. To learn about anything, one has to try hard and exert much effort. For example, even if you and your father had chattered for a hundred years hoping that I would quit my sojourn in Aleppo and Damascus, do you suppose I would have just returned? No, not until you came carrying 400 dinars [for traveling expenses], braving and

tolerating the hardships and dangers of the road and risking your livelihood, would I consider coming back. (Movahed 2009, 53)

During the long journey back, Shams and Sultan Valad conversed uninterruptedly, and Shams shared many valuable spiritual insights with his young devotee. There were many days of celebration following Shams's return to Konya, and Rumi, convinced that his disciples would now begin to appreciate Shams for the first time, brought Shams into his own household: "This time you shall take advantage of Shams ed-Din's words with greater appreciation, because the sail of the ship of man's being is belief. Where there's a sail the wind carries you to grand places, but if there's no sail words replace the wind." (Sâheb-Zamâni 1990, 47)

SHAMS AND KIMIA

As Rumi and Shams took up their private conversations again, the disciples realized that once more Rumi had chosen Shams over them, and soon their mistreatment of Shams started anew. Surely Rumi was painfully aware of their behavior, at least to some extent, and, perhaps hoping to hook Shams to Konya for good, he suggested marriage to Kimia. The young girl was the daughter of one of his followers who had suffered an untimely death and whose wife and children Rumi had brought into his own household to look after. Encouraged by Rumi, Shams married Kimia in November or December 1247 (Lewis 2000, 184), and Rumi allocated a quarter in his household to them.

Shams indeed grew deeply fond of Kimia, and they spent a blissful six months together during which she learnt much from his wisdom. It is believed, however, that Kimia was also dear to Rumi's middle son, Allaedin. Allaedin, unlike Sultan Valad, was not too keen on Shams to begin with, and when Shams married Kimia, according to some sources, his jealousy and antagonism escalated. He frequently came and went in Rumi's household and thus had an opportunity to see Kimia often; this angered Shams, who told him off one day, implying that he was not welcome.

Unwilling to accept that he was being turned away from his own father's home by the uncouth Shams, Allaedin and his friends were reinvigorated in their animosity, and their verbal lashings of the "old man" were taken to unprecedented heights. The jealousy and slander of Shams even extended to insinuations that Shams had indulged in forbidden acts:

"Is drinking wine forbidden?"

"Depends on who's drinking! It's like pouring a container of wine into the sea, where it would not change the sea at all, it would not pollute the water, and drinking and doing ablutions with it would be fine. However, if you pour just a few drops of wine into a small pool, undoubtedly it will infest all of the water. It is similar to when you drop something into a salty sea; that object becomes completely salt ridden. Thus the straight answer to your question, whether it's all right for Mowlânâ Shams ed-Din to drink wine, is that it's completely permissible, as his nature is like that of the sea. But, for *you*, even barley bread is not all right!" replied Rumi. (Sâheb-Zamâni 1990, 38)

Shams was firm in his reasons for being in Konya, and, despite the unforgiving behavior of Rumi's followers, he continued with his usual manner of dealing with those who literally hated him, reminding them: "When you hurt me, you are hurting Mowlânâ in turn" (Mova-hed 2009, 175).

Not long after they were married, one day Kimia accompanied the other ladies of the household on an outing to one of Konya's famous gardens without asking for Shams's permission. Upon her return, Shams rebuked her sharply. Shams, of course, was a traditional Muslim male with traditional views about women. In one instance, he admits:

> If Fatimah, the Prophet's daughter, or Ayshe, his wife, were to become shaykhs, I would lose faith in Mohammad, but they didn't! Even if God were to open a door for a woman, she should remain silent and hidden. A woman's place is in the corner of a room behind the spindle, where she should occupy herself with looking after the one who is her keeper. (Modaress-Sâdeghi 1994, 215)

Sadly, it happened that Kimia fell ill the very evening after returning from the outing, never to recover again. In his *Maghâlât,* Shams mentions that in Kimia, he had seen the face of God, and that's why he loved and appreciated her so dearly. He also mentions that he was not averse to family life and would have liked to have had a son by Kimia. His heart must have been shattered by her untimely death. The behavior of Rumi's *morīds,* however, did not abate even after the loss of Kimia, and Rumi's hopes that they would at last understand and begin to appreciate Shams were soon dissipated.

SHAMS DISAPPEARS

Shortly following Kimia's death, Shams disappeared for a second and final time from Konya and from Rumi's life, but we cannot be certain of the exact date or the manner of his disappearance. Rumi specialists have argued at length about various possible scenarios of Shams's disappearance, most of which speculate that he may have been murdered, but there is no evidence that any of these lurid tales could be true. In fact, there is no mention of murder in any of Rumi's subsequent poems or those of his son Sultan Valad. In fact, Rumi traveled to Syria at least twice in search of Shams in the years that followed his vanishing, which clearly indicates that he did not accept that Shams was dead.

A number of stories have been told about Shams's disappearance, some of which may hold a kernel of truth, while others, like most stories told about Shams and Rumi, are just embellished tales. One of the most popular accounts is that Shams was murdered by Allâedin and his friends. It has also been argued that Allâedin's dislike of Shams was triggered not out of jealousy over Kimia but because of Shams's preference for Sultan Valad, his older brother. Allâedin had high hopes of inheriting his father's mantle, but Shams, as long as he was still in the picture, was making it impossible for him to achieve this.

In this story, we are told that one evening, as Shams and Rumi are sitting together, there's a knock on the door, and Shams is called outside. Before he steps out of the room, he turns to Rumi and says that he must leave, because his tormentors are calling him to his death! As he is then stabbed by Alláedin and his friends, he lets out a heart-wrenching cry that frightens the murderous party unconscious. When they come to, they see no sign of Shams other than a few drops of blood!

In a different story, we are told that seven blood-thirsty *darvishes* from a different sect who had been look-ing for Shams for years, blaming him for the demise of their shaykh, finally find him in Konya and send him a message asking him to meet them outside town in an abandoned caravansary. Shams willingly goes to meet with them, knowing that he will be murdered. Each *darvish* strikes Shams once, and only with the last blow is Shams brought to his knees. It is highly unlikely that these stories hold any truth, as the murderous act would have been almost impossible to hide in a relatively small town as Konya, especially since it involved Rumi's beloved Shams.

A different version of these stories suggests that, after murdering Shams, his assailants throw his corpse down a well; afterward, the body is retrieved by Sultan Valad and a few *morīds* and unceremoniously buried, the facts hidden from Rumi. Why would Sultan Valad do such a thing—in the dark of the night, digging an unmarked grave, then keeping it from his father—especially seeing his father's unrelenting sorrow at the loss of his companion? The story is hardly credible. In addition, how could he then allow his father to bear the suffering of two long and fruitless trips to Syria in search of Shams, knowing that the man was already dead and buried?

These scenarios, dreamed up by various writers many years after the actual disappearance of Shams, must have been intended to dramatize the already incredible story of two men who had found spiritual love but who could not convince others of the simplicity of their revelation.

Shams's disappearance is more likely to have resulted from his realization that he had nothing more to teach Rumi; true to form, he chose to leave quietly without telling his friend, knowing that Rumi would try to convince him to stay. Some commentators have simply concluded that Shams was fed up with the verbal and occasional physical abuse he received, especially after Kimia's death, and that he just picked up and left!

Certainly, some combination of these two scenarios makes more sense than the murder theories. No evidence of Shams's remains has ever been found. It has never been proven that he was buried in Maghâm-e Shams in Konya, where a modern-day mosque has been erected around a grave thought to be his, or in Khuy in Azarbaijân Province, believed due to the finding of a minaret dated to the same era. No murder weapon was ever found. Therefore, we might like to simply accept that "Flying Shams" took his last flight out of popular sight, never to be seen again. We cannot be totally sure but can only assume that the date of his disappearance was in late 1247 or very early 1248.

THE END AND THE BEGINNING

The result of the mixing of these two great seas of spiritual wisdom is Rumi's extensive books of mystical poetry—the six volumes of the *Masnavi-ye Ma'navi;* the *Divan-e Shams-e Tabrizi;* his discourses, or *Fihe ma Fih;* and the *Maktubât,* or letters—and from Shams, a single volume, the *Maghâlât.* In the roughly two and a half years that Shams and Rumi spent together, many of the subjects they covered as found in the *Maghâlât* later appear in Rumi's verse, especially the *Masnavi* and *Fihe ma Fih.*

To name a few instances, Shams tells the story of the *samâzan,* in which the caliph bans the *samâ;* Rumi uses the last line in a different story in *Masnavi* 3 (v. 4707). Shams relates the poem "I shall not place you in my heart . . . ," and Rumi fashions the same verse as a quatrain (v. 1861). Shams briefly talks about the joy of encountering an elephant, while Rumi devotes an entire story to this theme called "The Elephant in the Dark" in *Masnavi* 3 (v. 1259), as he does Shams's story about the mouse and the camel in *Masnavi* 2 (v. 3436).

Shams briefly advises that it's best to stop trying to swim and instead to let the sea carry you; Rumi tells this parable in a much longer version in *Masnavi* 3 (v. 2841). Shams retells the story of why the Prophet refrained from saving the masses from ignorance; Rumi himself retells it in *Masnavi* 3 (v. 2913). Shams briefly tells the story of the three companions sharing halva, and Rumi retells it elaborately in *Masnavi* 6 (v. 2376).

Shams complains how some shaykhs are not genuine and alludes to a story about cats and mice; Rumi covers the same subject in *Masnavi* 6 (v. 3042). Shams tells the humorous story about an older man who goes to the barber asking him to cut only his white hairs; Rumi relates the story just as briefly in *Masnavi* 3 (v. 1376). Shams compares himself to duck eggs under a sitting hen; Rumi recasts the analogy as a story in *Masnavi* 2 (v. 3764).

In many cases, Rumi adheres to Shams's way of recounting a story as far as poetic rhyme and beat allow, but Rumi's storytelling is different from Shams's. Whereas Shams tells a story in a few sentences, Rumi embellishes it and extends it to numerous pages, sometimes to the extent that the original plot is buried in detail and forgotten.

For example, the story of Nassouh comprises more than 100 verses; the story of Ayaz and Mahmood is told in 130 verses; and the story of the poor man who finds a treasure is told in more than 500 verses (Movahed 2008, 157). Although Shams tells his stories briefly, he covers the subject matter precisely and efficiently, without much embellishment; when the story is lengthy, he never indulges in introducing extra subjects and thus diluting the original storyline.

One example, however, in which Shams tells a story at great length, but Rumi finishes it in just a few verses is the story of Leily and Majnoun in *Masnavi* 1 (v. 407). In his stories, Shams tries to demonstrate specific human behavior; for example, how different religious groups impose their own understanding of Islam on their followers and do not reveal the original message of the Prophet. He also stresses the fact that each group believes that paradise is his or her own realm, while others who are not members of the same clan do not deserve entry. No one in fact wants to see others who are not part of their own group enjoy the fruits of their labor; this tendency regretfully lingers in the 21st century as it did in the 13th.

Four important concepts that both Rumi and Shams dwell on extensively are:

1. Celebration of Life
2. Compassionate Interpretation of Death
3. Trust in Human Values and Their Infinite Possibilities
4. Call to Happiness, Joy, and Cheerfulness

We see Shams celebrating life when he says:

I am surprised at the hadith which claims that the world is the prison of the pious, while the grave is their safe house and paradise—their eternal resting place—while, for the infidel, the world is his paradise, the grave is a torture chamber, and hell is his throne! I personally have seen nothing but joy, greatness, and abundance in this life! (Movahed 2009, 154)

Shams loved and respected life, even as he did not fear death, considering the latter to be just another phase in man's spiritual journey, a passage to God: "Warriors of God seek death as much as poets seek the verse, the sick seek health, prisoners seek freedom, and children, holidays!" (Movahed 2009, 72). Shams trusted human values and believed in the infinite possibility of human growth and the search for perfection:

One must always try to achieve more, do more praying, seek more knowledge, and become a better Sufi, a perfect mystic! Ask more of everything for whatever exists in the world also exists in man. (Movahed 2009, 99)

Both Shams and Rumi were great champions of joy and happiness, and their Sufism stemmed from these concepts: they considered human beings to be the center of God's world. To understand Shams is to understand Rumi; without one another, they would not each be such provocative and important personalities who have beautifully infiltrated our consciousness, guiding us on our own spiritual paths. To read Shams's own words is to bring his consciousness even closer to ours, allowing us to finally appreciate the man who literally sacrificed himself for the sake of his love.

THE SAYINGS OF SHAMS

All of these sayings have been taken from *Khomi az Sharab e Rabani,* an abridged version of the *Maghâlât,* and have been gathered by Mohammad-Ali Movahed.

1

The mirror never lies. You can lie prostrate before it, begging a hundred times to conceal a fault, but it will only stare silently back.

2

You speak of the glory of God, but who are *you* and what do *you* have to offer? You speak of the wisdom of saints, but what have *you* achieved? I speak from my own experience; I do not use other people's words. Speak only if you have something of value to say. When your own ideas become clear, you may argue your point, and only then can you use the wisdom of others for support.

3

While men turn whirling in *samâ,* God manifests and reveals Himself more clearly to them. They have succeeded in venturing beyond the world they know, but God elevates them even beyond other worlds yet unknown and connects them with the divine.

4

Prophets embody each other. Jesus tells the Jews: "You have not understood Moses well; come and see me so that you may fully appreciate him."

Mohammad says to Christians and Jews: "You have not understood Moses or Jesus properly; come to me so that you may get to know them better."

In turn, the Prophet Mohammad is asked: "Who will proclaim you, since you are the last of all the great prophets?"

"Those who have come to know themselves shall be my representatives, for only when one truly knows oneself will one know God."

5

The more erudite you are, the farther you are from the goal. The more complicated one's thoughts, the more distant one grows. Spirit work is the work of the heart, not the mind!

6

A man once found a letter directing him to a treasure. He was instructed to leave town from a certain gate, where he would see a mound. Standing with his back to the mound and facing Mecca, he was advised to shoot an arrow, and where it landed, the treasure would be lying beneath. He did as the letter instructed, over and over again, until he had no strength left, but he could find nothing.

Word got to the king, who immediately sent his marksmen to try for the treasure. Needless to say, they too found nothing. Helpless and frustrated, the first man appealed to God many times and eventually had a revelation: Was I told to pull the bowstring?

The man placed the bow on the string and let it simply fall to the ground. When he dug into the ground, he found the treasure right there under his feet. When God decides to bestow a favor, one needs to take just one step forward and the destination will be visible. In this case, what connection was there between initiating action and achieving the goal? Where was asceticism, where austerity? Those who had shot their bow farther were further from their goal and were denied the treasure altogether.

It is said that man is only one step away from finding the "treasure," and what could that "treasure" possibly be other than knowing oneself? Indeed, when you finally come to know yourself, you have found the eternal Treasure!

7

A man was talking about fish, when another man admonished him: "Keep quiet, what do you know of fish? Why do you speak of something you've no idea about?"

"What are you talking about? Are you implying that I don't know what a fish is?" the man retorted.

"No, you don't have a clue. If you do, then why don't you describe it?"

"The sign of a fish is that it has two horns just like a camel."

"I knew that you knew nothing about fish, but now I know that you can't even differentiate between a camel and a cow!"

8

Many years ago, a caliph banned the *samâ*. Upon hearing the decree, a *darvish*, a Sufi mystic who was a *samâzan* or whirler, suddenly fell ill. A physician was brought to his side who examined him thoroughly but could not find the cause of his illness. Soon afterward, the *darvish* passed away and the doctor performed an autopsy, finding a lump that had turned into an agate. The doctor kept the stone for a rainy day. And so, with time, the agate was sold and passed from hand to hand until it came to the very same caliph who had banned the *samâ*, who unknowingly had the stone set to a ring. Years later, he lifted the ban and decided to attend a whirling session himself. While turning, he noticed that his garment was soaked in blood, but couldn't find an injury anywhere on his body. He saw the ring on his finger glowing red hot as burning coal. He immediately sent his attendants to find the man who had sold him the stone, intending to trace the original owner. Eventually the search led to the physician, who recounted the story of the dying *darvish*, whose last words were: "When you notice drops of blood on the path, you can be sure that they have bled from my eyes!"

9

I have nothing to do with the masses, it's not for them that I've come; it's for the sake of those who guide people to God. I've come to put my finger on their *jugular vein!*

10

If someone comes to hear me talk in the manner of a shaykh or a Sufi master, or to debate with me or hear me tell him stories from the Koran, he will neither hear anything useful nor benefit from me in any way. But if he approaches me with "need" in his heart and yearning to gain insight, he will prosper. Otherwise, if he spoke for one day or for ten, or even for a hundred years, I shall stare at him with my fist under my chin only pretending to be listening to him.

11

Until you give yourself up completely to your task, it seems most difficult, even impossible. But the minute you give yourself unconditionally, the difficulties vanish altogether.

12

What is meant by "rule" or *velâyat?* Does it refer to the domain of a man with large armies and many regions and cities under his rule? No! The one who truly rules is he who can rule over his own ego, his state of mind, his personality, his speech, his silence, his anger, and his mercy. This is not to be like the *jabrī* or fatalists, who claim that they're helpless and that only God is capable, but to take responsibility for all aspects of your Self. You must maintain your silence when silence is required, speak when it's needed, show your anger when it's appropriate, and exercise your kindness and mercy when it's necessary. If you cannot control your own behavior, you shall be forever victimized by it, and your uncontrolled actions will impose their rule over you.

13

Like a mirror, my words are clear, and if you possess the imagination, the illumination to desire death, well done and congratulations to you! Please don't forget to keep us in your prayers, too. And should you lack such light and imagination, then seek them and be prepared to take a leap! If you are honest, why should you fear death?

14

A group had gathered around a dead beast, holding their noses, turning their backs on the corpse in disgust. A shaykh walked by and, unbothered by the stench, he looked at the dead animal with interest. Curious, the crowd asked him what was he looking at.

"I'm amazed to see what fine white teeth it has!"

A good man does not complain, nor does he dwell on finding faults with others. Take the one who complains by the throat and squeeze it, for certainly the fault lies with *him*.

15

I shall not place you in my heart
For you may get hurt by its wounds.
I won't keep you in my eyes
For I may belittle you and
expose you to the ridicule of common men.
I will hide you inside my soul,
not in my heart or in my eyes,
so that you may become one with my breath.

16

Take notice whether you are a distant friend who is close or a close friend who is distant.

17

"The arena of speech is vast. Everyone can say what they choose," exclaimed Shaykh Mohammad, better known as Ibn Arabi.

I said: "In fact, the arena of speech is rather limited! The arena of 'meaning' is limitless. Reach beyond words and you may see infinity."

18

If you stop obsessing over your own goodness and purity and correct all the mischief that you've committed up to now, the little goodness and purity that you indeed possess will increase manifold!

19

His silence does not germinate from ignorance, but from knowing too much!

20

The musician who's not in love, or the preacher who's never felt pain, will arouse only coldness in their audiences, thus quelling their ultimate purpose to create warmth and enthusiasm.

21

The problem among friends and people in general is that they don't look out for each other. We must live such that looking after friends is our constant occupation, as if we were inseparable from them!

22

Sufi shaykhs taught their students about the nature of "veils." They instructed about the seven hundred veils of darkness and seven hundred veils of light that cover the truth, according to the sayings of the Prophet. The poor students shivered in fright, unable to grasp the essence of the matter. These teachers thus lost their students because they robbed them of all hope. All veils are one and the same: the veil of the self!

23

Your true self is the one who shows his need! The one who pretended to be needless and a stranger is your enemy; that's why I was torturing him, because he was not the real you. How could I ever hurt you, when I think that if I try to lay a kiss on your feet I am constantly worried that my eyelashes might scratch and blemish your skin?

24

I desire nothing other than the need of the one who's in need. It is a requirement and a necessity for a spiritual student to donate his riches, to relieve himself of his attachment to the world, and to sit with an open heart before his shaykh.

25

The great caliph Haroun al-Rashid had heard about the love story of Leily and Majnoun and was curious to find out who this girl was that the whole world was talking about. Sparing no cost, he sent his men in search of the famous Leily so he could see her beauty firsthand. After much investigation and searching, the soldiers found Leily and brought her to the palace. During the night when she was asleep, the caliph went to her bedside and watched her closely for a long time. Perplexed, he wondered what Majnoun could possibly have seen in her. He thought perhaps that if he heard her speak, he might grasp something of her charm, so he decided to wake her up.

"Are you Leily?"

"Yes, I am Leily, but you are not Majnoun! You do not behold me with Majnoun's eyes! You must look at me the way Majnoun looks at me. The beloved must be regarded with her lover's eyes."

The problem is that people do not look upon God with love; they look at Him through the filters of science, philosophy, and reason. The workings of love are different!

26

A proud man asked to hear my secrets, so I told him: "I cannot tell you anything, for I can only reveal my secrets to someone in whom I see myself and not that other person. I tell my secrets only to myself! I do not see myself in you, I see another person!

"There are three ways in which one man can approach another: one is to become his student, another is to become a companion, and the last is to be a master. Now tell me, which one are you?"

27

My words will seem bitter to some, but if they can tolerate them, their sweetness will become apparent in the end. When you see someone who's happy even while devastated by bitterness, this is because they focus on the sweetness that awaits them in the end. Thus, the meaning of patience is to be able to see the end result, while impatience is the inability to extend one's vision to the future. Undoubtedly the ultimate winner is the one who can perceive the goodness in the end.

28

The essential purpose of a devotee is to find a shaykh who has a perfect vision of spiritual life and to grow close to him so as to learn from his traits, to learn to emulate him. Without doubt, by mingling with another, you'll take on his nature. If you stare endlessly at a heap of hay, you'll soon feel withered and dry; but if you focus on flowers and living plants, you'll be feeling fresh and alive. The one you socialize with will pull you into his world. That's why it's said that reading the Koran will cleanse one's heart: one is accompanied by saints and prophets, one inhabits the state in which they lived, and consequently their memory will leave an imprint on one's soul, becoming one's constant companion.

29

I was a theologian and diligently studied the canon. I now hardly remember any of it, unless suddenly it reveals itself to me of its own accord, because I no longer have the head to recall it.

30

I care about a great many masters, but I will no longer show my affection for them, because a couple of times I did and they neither understood nor appreciated me. I tolerate them, so that the little affection they feel does not wither. With Mowlânâ, however, I did reveal myself, and my love did not suffer but increased manifold. I cannot always tell the truth with everyone, for if I do they may turn me away, and if I tell the whole truth the entire town will chase me out.

31

The world is a bad place for a person who doesn't understand it! Once he discovers the world properly, it will no longer have a hold over him. He might ask: "What is the world?"

"It's not the afterlife," he's told.

"What is the afterlife?"

"Tomorrow."

"What is tomorrow?"

Indeed, the arena of language and words is difficult and utterly limited. The seeker asks questions hoping to escape from the restricted world of language, but he gets twisted up in it even more with every new question.

32

Just talking knowledgeably about an issue does not make it possible. To learn about anything, one has to try hard and exert much effort. For example, even if you and your father had chattered for a hundred years hoping that I would quit my sojourn in Aleppo and Damascus, do you suppose I would have just returned? No, not until you came carrying 400 dinars [for traveling expenses], braving and tolerating the hardships and dangers of the road, and risking your livelihood, would I consider coming back.

33

You have many obstacles in your way! Money for most is their Mecca, but the great masters have loosened its claws, and it no longer holds a grip on them. On the other hand, for those who are in love with the world, money is more precious than their sweet life, as if they were not even alive—because if they were, how could money be dearer?

34

Measurements vary from hand to hand and from knee to knee. You do not possess the same standards as Mohammad. You've allowed the pharaoh of your ego to take over your soul and have lost hold of the Moses of your spirit; they come and go without your permission, and you have no control over either of them. Hold on to Moses so that pharaoh can never return. This dithering between right and wrong will not benefit you in the long run.

35

Stains on the soul must be wiped clean; even a speck inside will cause more harm than a thousand stains on the outside. What kind of water could possibly wash off that inner stain? Perhaps a few water skins filled with tears, and they must be honest tears. After cleansing, a penitent can anticipate safety and protection; finally, he can sleep peacefully.

36

Tears and prayers that don't embrace Spirit will carry you as far as your grave, but not beyond it. Only tears and prayers that have been steeped in need and longing will stay with you until the day of resurrection, and further on to paradise and even to God's own lap. The heart filled with need for Spirit is always awake; if not, it will be sleeping in the path of an oncoming flood.

37

Two men were traveling together as part of a group. One of them had a belt filled with gold coins, which he never parted with. The other man anxiously waited for the gold owner to fall asleep so he could rob him. The owner of the gold innately slept lightly, and the thief could never outwit him. They arrived at the last resting place before their destination, and the thief, who had lost all hope of his prize and thinking that he might as well make a joke of it, asked the man: "Why don't you ever sleep?"

"Why should I?"

"So I can strike you in the head with a rock and steal your gold!"

"Really? Now with this hope in my heart I can finally sleep peacefully."

38

Everyone praises his or her own shaykh, but the Prophet himself initiated me in my sleep! He gave me an initiation robe unlike any other, not one that ages after two days and can be thrown into the furnace of the bathhouse, or that you can clean yourself with after you've gone to the toilet! It is a robe of spiritual conversing, and not the sort of conversation that can be understood with one's mind but one that is timeless, that transcends yesterday, today, and tomorrow! What can love possibly have to do with today and tomorrow, anyway?

39

A mouse happened to come by the reins of a camel; he grasped the reins in his teeth and proudly began to lead him around. The camel, unbeknown to the mouse, had been disobedient before God and, feeling guilty and downtrodden, allowed the mouse to lead him, thinking that this was surely God's will. Meanwhile, the mouse imagined that it was his own might that had over-whelmed the camel, and he ordered him: "Walk on, I shall lead you."

The camel soon noticed that they were about to reach a body of water, and he stopped. The mouse exclaimed: "Why are you stalling?"

"There's a wide stream before us; allow me to see how deep it is. Stand back."

The camel checked the depth of the water, stepped back, and told the mouse: "It's easy, come, it's just up to my knee."

"Yes, I can see that, but there's a difference between your knee and mine!"

"Have you repented now to never be insolent again? And if you ever are, then display your insolence with one who has the same knee height as yourself!" the camel said coyly.

"I've repented, I've repented," repeated the mouse. "Now take me on your back please!"

The camel knelt down to allow the mouse to climb onto his hump. He said: "If there's a stream, the River Jeyhoun, or even the greatest sea ahead, have no fear; I will carry you forever because I'm fearless!"

40

Until they learn to trust me unconditionally and respect me in public, I shall be harsh with my friends. They ask, why am I kind to strangers and unkind to them? I simply ask them in turn, can they not see my undying kindness toward them? I also tell them that if the great saints in all their glory were alive and could see us together, their fondest wish would be to sit with us for a moment! I'm harshest toward those I love most, but it's only so that they'll give up their antagonism and distrust, so that I can make them privy to my secrets. Antagonism and distrust have no place among God's creations.

41

I am all light and brightly shining from within! I was a funnel of water turning around myself, coming to a boil, swirling and creating a stench until Mowlânâ found me. Now I am flowing steadily, fresh, new, and content.

42

The *morīd* is not immune to the temptations of the world until his training is complete, and therefore he needs to be near his shaykh. One cold breath blown onto him can turn him icy cold, like a deadly poison such as the exhalation of a dragon, which blackens everything it breathes upon. Once the novice has completed his training and is considered ready and well cooked, there's no longer any harm in his separation from his mentor.

43

Should a veil rise between the *morīd* and his shaykh and darkness descend upon him, at that hour he must pray more fervently that the veil be lifted. As the darkness increases and the shaykh fades from clear view, the student must redouble his efforts. He mustn't despair when the darkness is lengthened; in time, the light will reappear, and its duration shall be longer too.

44

Most residents of the underworld are clever; some among them are philosophers and scholars who hide behind their sagacity like a mask. Like the corrupt tribe of Yajouj, sometimes they say there's no path ahead and sometimes they say there's a road but it's difficult and too far. Indeed, the destination is far, but once you start the journey, you'll be so ecstatic that you won't feel the distance. Fields of colorful flowers and lush trees surround the arena of hell, but you can smell its foul scent rising and coming your way, polluting your beautiful road. The Garden of Eden, however, is surrounded by an orchard of thorns, but you can detect the scent of paradise that wafts toward you, carrying news of the lovers inside and transforming the thorns into objects of beauty.

45

If a person who is incapable of swimming, even if he has the strength of a lion, falls into the sea and begins to kick and splash around wildly, the sea will devour him, for this is the sea's custom. It will pull down the live one until he drowns and perishes, and once he's gone, the sea will become his carrier. However, if this same person lies still upon the water as though dead, the sea will not suck him under. Now, make yourself dead from the beginning, so that you may float on the waves in the sea.

46

My being is the alchemy that needs no pouring over copper; for me, just being present transforms the copper into gold. This is perfect alchemy!

47

"Why didn't you save the masses from the darkness of ignorance?" the Prophet was asked.

"Some sufferings cannot be alleviated. There are some illnesses for which the physician's care is useless, while there are others that can be cured, and it would be a sin not to care for them," he replied.

48

When the enemy has conquered and occupied a fort, it is imperative and honorable to attack and destroy it. To attempt to build and make the fort prosper under enemy rule is a sin, equivalent to treason. Once the fort is reconquered and the king's standard has again been raised, it is in turn disloyal and seditious to try to destroy it, while to rebuild it and make it flourish is essential and rendering a service.

49

To speak while in company of a learned speaker is bad manners, unless you are capable of offering a novel insight. It's like taking cash to the money exchange agent, asking him to separate the fake from the real notes!

50

Every instance of dishonesty and corruption in the world has resulted from someone imitating someone else, either copying them or refuting them. Imitation causes a person to blow hot and cold, as he encounters something different every day. If on one occasion he were to come across the truth and wish to change his mind about a matter he had equivocated about earlier, he must hide it, for people will know that he has been imitating others until then. He won't reveal anything, because he risks losing people's trust as well as all self-confidence in himself.

51

Were you able to do something such that I didn't have to go away for your benefit and we could attain what is necessary without the need for travel, it would indeed be worthwhile, for I am unable to order you to go away. I shall, therefore, take it upon myself to endure the trouble of traveling, because separation matures one. While separated from each other, one begins to think about all the things that one should have said openly, and how easy it would have been to be straightforward instead of saying everything in puzzles in an effort to avoid discord. It would have been so much easier than tolerating the hardships of travel and being separated. If need be I will take fifty trips for your sake, for what does it matter to me if I go away or not! It is all for your improvement; otherwise, what difference does it make if I were in Rûm or in Damascus, in Mecca or in Istanbul? It makes no difference to me, other than certainly traveling matures the person in many ways.

52

Eblīs, or the devil, can appear in the veins of man at any time, but never in the words of a *darvish,* for the *darvish* is not the speaker. He has been dissolved in God; he's in a state of *fanâ,* or nothingness, and is a *fâni,* or nothing, and no longer exists. His words come from the other side. It's like having a windpipe made of goatskin; when you blow into it, the sound it makes is not that of the goat but it's yours, for the goat, apart from an insignificant remnant of skin, is long gone. The *darvish* does not teach his own thoughts, for he's empty of himself and has been graced by God to deliver His messages.

53

"How far is God from us?"
    "As far as you are from God!"

54

The mind will lead you to the door but never into the house, for inside, reasoning is a veil, the mind is a veil, even the heart is a veil!

55

Speaking with the ignorant is extremely harmful, even forbidden by religion—it's harâm! To eat the food of the ignorant is forbidden, and if I were ever to attempt it, it would be hard to swallow—it would stick in my throat!

56

You criticize the idol worshipper for praying to an object, or to a wall that he has painted. You, too, turn to a wall and worship! This is the secret of Mohammad, which you do not comprehend. The Kaaba, the house of God, is positioned in the middle of the world, and people turn toward it from all sides. Were the Kaaba to be removed from the center, everyone would be facing each other, prostrating themselves before each other's hearts!

57

I was never in the habit of writing anything down. When I don't note down my thoughts, they stay with me, and every moment reveals them in a new light!

58

With us, no one becomes a Muslim on first effort! One swings between belief and disbelief many times, and every time one finds a new insight, until one is made complete.

59

I don't accept *morīd*s; I take shaykhs instead, and not just any shaykh but the perfect one!

60

A farmer was plowing his field when a passerby saw him, and, unable to differentiate between building and destroying, the passing stranger complained:

"Why are you turning over this healthy field?"

The man had no clue that if the soil is not toiled over, nothing will grow, and the land will rot. Is it not true that in order to build something new, the old must first be overhauled?

61

Blessed be the one whose eyes are asleep but whose heart is wide awake. Woe to him whose eyes are awake but whose heart always sleeps!

62

What a joy to see the elephant in its entirety! Though each limb is itself amazing, to see the whole carries another level of joy!

63

Bâyazid, the great Sufi, was on his pilgrimage to Mecca, and, as it was his custom every time he entered a new town, he would first pay his respect to the shaykhs of that town and afterward tend to his other affairs. He arrived in Basra and visited one of the shaykhs, who asked about his destination.

"I'm headed for the House of God in Mecca."

"What are you carrying as provisions for the journey?" asked the *darvish*.

"Two hundred dinars," answered Bâyazid.

"Get up and walk around me seven times, then give me your silver! Where do you think you're going, O great Bâyazid? It's true that the Kaaba is the house of God, and so is my heart. I swear to you that since the Kaaba was constructed, God has not set foot in there, and from the day that my heart was conceived it has never been empty of Him!"

Bâyazid leapt to his feet and laid the silver coins before the shaykh.

64

"God do this! God don't do that!" the chap keeps repeating, like he's ordering the King to do domestic work! He's turning the King into his servant!

65

A certain kind of poverty will take you to God and make you shun everything that is not entirely of Him; another kind of poverty will make you turn your back on God and find false comfort with the unenlightened masses.

Where a flower does not grow, a thorn will take its place.

Where there's no altar, there will be a gallows instead.

66

I have no awareness of my own head or beard, which are the closest things to me; how can I possibly be aware of you?

67

When someone has potential for spiritual achievement, prophets and saints will facilitate its flow and open the way for him, but when there's no potential, what's there to facilitate?

68

The secrets of divine messengers are hidden from the common man; that is why they try to study their writings instead. But each person makes his own interpretation and then ends up condemning the messengers. People never condemn their own interpretations or admit that they might be wrong, but always lay the blame on the written words.

69

The calligrapher wrote out three scripts: the first he could read, but no one else could; the second, both he and others could read; but the third, neither he nor anyone else could decipher. That third script is I!

70

A defendant in court was asked to provide witnesses, so he brought in ten Sufis. Upon seeing them, the judge asked him to bring yet another witness.

"My lord, I have brought you ten good witnesses, and you still ask for one more?"

"Even if you had brought a hundred thousand Sufis, they would all count as one!"

71

I'm fond of infidels because they don't pretend to be my friend. They admit that they are nonbelievers, that they are my enemy. I can teach them friendship and how to become one with me. The one who pretends to be my friend but is not, is the real enemy!

72

When I am joyful, even if the whole world were steeped in sorrow, it would not affect me, and if I were sad, I would likewise never allow anyone to be affected by my sadness!

73

A *morīd* was criticizing another *morīd,* saying that he should not try to glean my secrets. I asked the first, how did he come to that conclusion? He said:

"He perpetually claims that things should be done in such and such a way! If he totally surrendered to you, how could he claim to know these things better than you?"

"So you don't consider your criticism to be the same as his when you say, 'This should be done this way, and that should be done that way'? Perhaps, then, what you say should also not be followed!"

This reminds me of the Indian chap who broke his prayer by speaking in the middle of praying, and another chap who was also praying likewise breaking his prayer to tell him off.

74

Friendship is finding your friend asleep, grabbing his covers and pulling them off, leaving him naked before all eyes, like Noah before his son, and putting a weapon to his darkened face, tearing off his veil of sleep! Friendship is not always about laughing and making merry, all the while afraid to cause offense. That is not kindness, nor is it true friendship.

75

The heart is greater than the sky and even more expansive than the celestial spheres; yet it is tender and delicate, bright and clear! Why do people constrict their heart with their thoughts and temptations, turning their lives into prison terms? What prudence is there, turning a beautiful garden into a dire jail? What's the sense in weaving a cocoon of adverse thoughts and provocations around one's own neck, imprisoning and suffocating oneself? I, however, turn that prison into a garden for my own benefit! Can you imagine, if my prison is a garden, what my garden must be like?

76

Why limit one's life with negative thoughts? Whatever the consequences, one must quickly share and discuss one's thoughts with friends, and so become free of them. Don't torture yourself about how to express your thoughts to your friend, for he probably already knows what you're thinking.

77

Most spiritual guides are hidden from us. People exaggerate when they say a certain person is all kindness! They presume that this is perfection; it is not! The one who is all kindness is in fact incomplete; it's not fair to say that God has only bestowed kindness on him. You are denying him the possibility of also possessing anger, even wrath. It's indeed necessary to have the capacity for both kindness and anger, but each in its own place. The ignorant one possesses both these capacities but doesn't know the right occasions in which to apply them, thus exposing these traits out of stupidity and lack of direction.

78

The whirling of men of God is *lateif*—delicate in nature, like a leaf floating on the surface of water. Inside, their movements are strong and sturdy like a pillar, yet on the outside they appear light as straw!

79

The chef spilled some food onto the king's robe! The king ordered him to be hanged. The chef then quickly dropped the rest of the platter onto the king's lap. The king thought this was funny and asked him why he did it.

"I didn't spill much at first, and since you ordered me to be hanged and I had nothing to lose, I thought I may as well spill the whole thing!"

80

The purpose of creation is for two friends to meet and sit before each other, to encounter God away from all temptations. The purpose of creation is not bread or the baker, meat or the butcher; it is all about this instance when I'm in the company of Mowlânâ!

81

On someone's gravestone it was inscribed that he had lived for only an hour! I would that, if my life were but an hour, it could be in service to Mowlânâ.

82

The self-aware man is he who is content even in times of sorrow, for he knows that hope is entwined with hopelessness. In despair there's hope, and in hope there is the sorrow of imminent despair! The day it was my turn to suffer with a high fever, I was happy in the knowledge that the following day would be pregnant with health. On the contrary, the day I was in best of health I knew that the time would come when I would suffer in turn.

83

Search for a lover to fall in love with, and if you don't completely fall for her, find another! There are many beautiful faces hidden behind their veils.

Three friends, a Muslim, a Christian, and a Jew were traveling together; they happened to come by a little money and decided to buy a sweet called halva with it. As it was quite late in the evening and there wasn't enough halva for all three of them, they decided that the one who had the best dream that night would get to eat the whole batch the next day, hoping to deny the Muslim his share. The Muslim, however, woke up in the middle of the night, as no lover who's been denied his beloved ever finds sleep, and polished off the entire halva.

The next morning the Christian recounted his dream: "I dreamt that Jesus descended from heaven and took me back with him."

The Jew boasted: "I dreamt that Moses carried me with him to paradise, and I noticed that you and Jesus were only dwindling in the fourth heaven! How can one compare the beauty of paradise with what you saw?"

The Muslim nonchalantly said: "Mohammad came and said to me: 'You poor fellow, one of them was taken to the fourth heaven and the other to paradise itself! You have been unfairly deprived; you deserve to eat the whole halva.' So I ate the whole thing!"

The other two agreed that his dream was the best, while theirs had been but vain fantasy.

85

When you embrace the gardener, the garden becomes yours, and you may pick from every tree.

86

God's promises are never unfulfilled.

87

You have become stale; that's why I seem stale to you! Look at me with new and fresh eyes, for I never age or become stale. Don't allow yourself to become old and stale either, and if you do suddenly start to feel older, search for the reason; think about whom you've been socializing with. Have you wasted away with those who are reined in by their temptations? What happened to you? Lay the blame on yourself! Reignite your longing; rejuvenate it, for I am already new. Prove yourself, for I am already proven and do not need your approval, and if you try to offer it, it's because of your own insecurity.

88

To be a *darvish* is to be forever silent.

89

Appearances are many and varied, but the essence is always one and the same. I recall Mowlânâ saying: "People are like a bunch of grapes such that each one can be singled out, but once they're squeezed into juice, can anyone distinguish them from each other?"

90

To read a thousand treatises on spirituality to a person who does not have the disposition to comprehend them is like burdening a donkey with a ton of books!

91

One day a preacher was giving a sermon from the pulpit: "I long for the company of someone with whom I can have substantial spiritual conversations."

A woman in the crowd stood up and took off her veil, uncovering her face. The preacher rebuked her and told her to sit down. She exclaimed:

"You are only a pretender and not a true holy man! Your words have no weight. You may wish to preach God's truth, but who are you to speak of His truth? It's not yours to speak about. On the day of resurrection there shall be no difference between man and woman; everyone will be the same before God's eyes!"

The preacher spoke no more.

92

These men who speak from the pulpits and lead the prayers are the thieves of our religion!

93

Mowlânâ is enough for me, but you must remember that while you may read the page facing you, you must also read your lover's side of the page, for it will benefit you greatly. All your suffering stems from the fact that you do not read what your lover has written on his side of the page.

94

Resurrection day is now! The veil of the unseen has been lowered and all is in view, but only for those who have untainted vision!

95

In *khâneghâhs,* or Sufi houses, the resident *darvishes* can't tolerate my presence. When I speak in schools, my words drive my students and colleagues crazy, and why should wise men lose their minds? With them I cannot speak, I can only say that I'm a Sufi! I'm not part of this Sufi house, which is filled with good men, but men who have no ability to buy their own food and cook it!

96

What is a shaykh? Existence, presence, being!
What is a *morīd?* Nothing!
Until the *morīd* becomes nothing,
he is not yet a *morīd.*

97

When someone encounters me, he will either become a true Muslim or a diehard atheist. Not comprehending my essence, he will only understand my outer form, thus finding fault with my superficial piety. Being ambitious, he will imagine that he too has no need to perform his prayers, thus losing out on all the advantages, all the benefits that ensue from praying.

98

Remember my will: never retell what I tell you. Never repeat my words. If people ask you to describe what you've heard, just say that it was pleasant and life giving but that you couldn't repeat it even if you tried. Ask them, if they need to hear me, why don't they come and listen to me themselves? When I see them, I will know whether I'd like to speak with them, whether they are worthy of it! Otherwise I'll just be silent.

99

Mowlânâ has been naturally blessed with unlimited spiritual knowledge and is not bound to share it with others. I, however, have been blessed with God's revelations since childhood and have been decreed to teach men in such a way that they'll be able to release themselves from the yoke of their egos and thus further improve their lives.

100

The masses believe that they should pray and fast more during special holy months because God will then look upon them more mercifully. How can that be? Can God not see at all times? Can He not hear and speak at all times? How can you say that He only sees His subjects' acts during the holy months, while the rest of the time you can drink and engage in immoral acts at will? How dare you claim that He cannot see because He's not here until the next holy month, so that you can bring out the wine and get drunk!

101

I was a jug of divine wine, with the top sealed, unknown by anyone. However, I lent my ears to the world and listened, and when the wine's seal was cracked open it was for the sake of Mowlânâ; whoever benefits from this wine owes it to him. I belong to Mowlânâ, and my only intention is to return the blessing back to him.

102

Prophets do not give you what you don't already have. They try to polish the mirror of your heart to wipe off the myriad shades that hide it. The sole purpose of their efforts is to lift your veils so that you may find the truth yourself!

103

The ignorant can only understand their own writing; they are unable to decipher anyone else's. Had they been able to comprehend even just one line of their friend's writing, they would not speak such nonsense! They have illusions; they grasp for the wrong concepts; they create idols for themselves and become their slaves!

104

"Mowlânâ is free of the world while Shams is not, but Mowlânâ tells us that, because we don't like Shams, we are quick to accuse him of pettiness and avarice," complained some students.

Little do they know that the approving eyes of love are unable to detect defects in those they love.

105

The eyes of kindness and love are unable to spot faults, while the eyes of anger and enmity can perceive only evil. To love means to be blind to any wrong, just like a mother who loves her child cannot reproach him for anything.

106

As Rumi defended Shams's position before his followers, Shams also had a word to add to his own defense: "Mowlânâ's words of support perhaps suffer from weakness, so let me tell you how it is. Someone ties up his limping donkey and feeds it hay day and night, but the beast shits on him every time. Another man rides his Arab horse, which continually whisks him to safety from countless bandits and other dangers and calamities on the road. Although Mowlânâ's already connected to the spiritual world, the horse plays a fair share in his spiritual advancement."

107

I bequest to Baha'edin [Sultan Valad], Rumi's elder son, three pieces of advice so that he may progress further in his quest of spirituality. He has all the good qualities he needs; for instance, if he should come by 100,000 dirhams, he would be sure to give it away instantly. Yet I would like to leave him with three wishes: First is to never lie, second is to not take any hashish (as some *darvishes* do), and third is to mingle less with his companions. But lying is the worst of all ills.

108

What a great difference there is between the person whose delight is sourced from his ego, the one who's found joy in his heart, and the third who can only find joy in God!

In a hadith, God spoke to Moses:

"O Moses, I was hungry, but you didn't feed me! What will you do if I come to your door again?"

"O God, you are above going to any door!"

"And what if I do?" God insisted. "I am indeed very hungry; prepare me some food and I shall return tomorrow."

The next day at sunrise, Moses began to prepare a variety of dishes; soon everything was ready to be served, except he didn't have enough water. A *darvish* happened to come to Moses's door at that moment asking for alms.

"You've arrived just in time!" said Moses, who proceeded to hand him two jugs to fill with water from the well.

"I will serve you a hundred times," said the *darvish;* he took the jugs, filled them with water, and then returned. Moses gave him a loaf of bread in return.

Having gone through a lot of trouble to create a feast for God, Moses now sat waiting. As the hours passed, there was no sign of God, so finally he distributed the food among his neighbors, wondering what the moral of this affair might possibly be. Did the secret lie in being gracious to his neighbors? Or was the intention to show his irrefutable submission to the Lord? This episode passed, until later Moses had a revelation and asked God:

"You ordered me to prepare You a meal, but You never came."

"I did come, but you didn't even give me a loaf of bread without making me bring you two jugs of water first!"

110

One dinar of Mowlânâ is worth a hundred dinars belonging to someone else, including his followers. If anyone ever finds himself at my side, it is due to Mowlânâ, for it's because of him that a closed door was at last opened! I am an expert at knowing Mowlânâ, for we speak openly and never hide what we mean. Every day I learn something new from his actions and his state of mind, something unknown to me before. You must learn to understand Mowlânâ much better so that you can end your condition of stagnation. Don't be satisfied with just the lovely words that come out of his lovely mouth; seek out what lies beyond them. Ask him to reveal to you what is hidden.

111

Mowlânâ has two types of teaching: one offers the truth in a straightforward way, while the other hides the meaning. All the saints wish that they were still alive today and could be privy to these truths.

112

A mule once asked a camel: "How come I always fall on my face and you hardly ever do?"

"When I reach a pass, I look around the corner to see what lies before me, because I'm tall and capable and have perfect vision. I take one look at the end of my view and one look at what's before my feet, and then take a step forward," replied the camel wisely.

113

There is a whirlpool that scares everyone except for one able swimmer! He's unwilling to save himself without helping others first. They may think that they're being pulled around by the whirlpool, unaware that the swimmer is there to save them. In every whirlpool, in every sea, there exists a narrow path of escape that has to be sought out in order to reach safety.

114

I speak of the great Treasure, and you're still hung up on a penny, afraid you'll lose it!

115

You may not own much, but do keep a little of what you have safe for my sake and hide it. The amount might be meager and I will certainly not become rich from it or become a poor *darvish* from lack of it, but it will open doors for you. One day suddenly you may experience grace from the spirit world, and then nothing of this world will matter anymore.

There are men who interrupt me and try to boast of their knowledge, like that Sharaf Lahâvari, the so-called mystic. He continued lecturing me on how saints are the recipients of messages from the spirit world and how for some the messages come regularly and how for some they appear only now and then. For God's sake, who are you to speak about saints in the first place? And if I turn away from him, he will complain that I am jealous of him, that I am his enemy! I have a habit of praying for Jews, so that they shall find guidance. I also pray for the one who curses me, hoping that God will show him a better occupation than cursing and that he may learn how to pray and become occupied with Spirit. How can Lahâvari even begin to imagine whether I'm a saint or not? What is it to him, I want to know? It's like when Jouhi, that farcical character, was told that people were carrying trays full of presents in the street, and he said: "What's it to me?" Jouhi's companion then said that the people were bringing the presents to his house, and he said: "What's it to you?"

117

When you gild the truth trying to hide its meaning, you may upset a few people, but most will be pleased and excited. If you're straightforward and do not conceal the truth, most will probably feel no excitement or enthusiasm, unless they've been gifted with the ability to hear and tolerate with pleasure the absolute truth.

118

A Sufi argued that at the beginning of one's spiritual journey, one must learn about mystic traditions and engage in debates, and afterward the path should be clear and walking it, simple. To which Shams replied:

"I have told you how to journey to the first station, but you didn't! Now you're asking me how to get to the next stations further down the road? I'm instructing you to start your journey, and I will accompany you to the first stop, after which you'll know for certain which way is safer. But you must make the journey to the first stop!"

119

Those who believe in the one and only God and have stood by their word have no fear of death. When they arrive at their graves, they shall see a host of lights, and the angel of death shall hold no fear for them. In fact, to them Azrael is an angel of life, for he shall free them from this dark and narrow existence that has been their prison.

120

They say that when men age they become like children; well, I tell them that does not apply to everyone. Saints and prophets do not behave in such a manner, and neither does Mowlânâ; nor did his revered father, who lived beyond the ripe age of eighty and every day became even more knowledgeable. Therefore, I reiterate that this statement is not true for everyone.

121

When they say "Blessings are bestowed by great men," what do they mean by "great?" Is it a reference to age or to other visible aspects, which are dependent on time and will inevitably decay? Or do they mean "great" when it comes to the essence in the sense of never-changing and ever-present?

122

Sometimes there's no other way but to keep silent and surrender!

123

True advantage lies in the fact that when you take a bite of food, you must wait until it's digested and has proffered all its goodness before you take the next bite. This is wisdom. Now it's a different story if someone is ill and suffering and desperately needs to consume his food quickly; such an afflicted person must not experiment with our kind of food. As for myself, when I first begin to study a science, until I have firmly grasped the essence of each lesson, I shall not begin a new one. There's no cause for criticism if a student has to read a subject many times in order to properly understand and internalize it. I will never begin a new subject with Mowlânâ unless I have fully understood his lesson of the day before. It is infinitely wiser to repeat and go over a theme many times, achieving genuine understanding, than to superficially study a thousand topics.

124

Pay attention and observe the precise moment when you experience the opening of your heart. For some, it's in coming to us; for others it's in going away. I wonder which it is for you?

> Be aware that you cannot trick Him into union.
> Milk from the jug of faith is not served to just any drunk.
> When the selfless gather round,
> Not even a sip is wasted on the selfish.

125

These people are right not to warm to my words, for my talk is great and mighty and challenges them. The Koran and the Prophet's words have been expressed to fulfill a need, and thus they make sense to people, while mine are uttered neither to meet a need nor to fulfill a yearning; they are so lofty that if you try to snatch them, you might lose your head!

126

People are mostly happy when lied to and sad when told the truth. I told someone that he was a great man, one of a kind in his time. He was delighted and took my hand and confessed that he had been wrong before and was now keen on keeping my company. Last year I told this same man the truth, and he turned against me! How strange! One has to live a lie with people in order to live happily among them. The moment one tells the truth, one must head for the desert, because it's impossible to survive among the gullible masses.

127

A group of people who had attained enlightenment claimed that because they had arrived at a high spiritual station, why should they continue to perform their prayers? I asked them that if they believed they had reached such an exalted state, would they not think that the Prophet had also attained it? And did he stop praying?

128

I was staying in a small room in a caravansary when someone asked me why I didn't stay at the *khâneghâh,* the Sufi house. I told him:

"I don't consider myself worthy of the *khâneghâh!* That place is for those who don't have the time to buy food and cook for themselves because their time is too precious. That's not me."

"Why don't you at least come to the school?"

"I'm not the type who can argue and debate. If I speak in my own way, they will mock me and accuse me of blasphemy. I'm a stranger, and a caravansary is more suitable for the likes of me!" I replied cunningly.

129

Difficulties arise when darkness descends upon the soul, creating veils and estrangement, allowing the ego to take over and concoct its own interpretations. In a space where there's love and light, the ego does not even begin to stir!

130

If they held the blazing light of faith in their hearts, how could they pay such hefty sums to buy their ranks and positions?

131

The grape that has not yet ripened must be kept safe from the cold and from excessive heat. Once it is sweetly ripened, a blazing sun will not harm it anymore and neither will the freezing snow. The same goes for the novice!

132

A man who has reached perfection is enveloped in light and is drunk on the pleasure of knowing the truth. When he's this drunk, how can he be expected to guide another person? Beyond this drunkenness is a state of awareness in which man's kindness overrides his anger. The man who's spiritually drunk but has not yet reached a state of perfection finds that his anger and mercy are equal. The one whose mercy supersedes his wrath, however, is fit to lead. God has kindness and wrath in equal measure, but His essence is all mercy, and it is this that prevails at all times. Thus, mercy is the ultimate victor.

133

The teachings of a shaykh are like rare walnuts, which are unerring and bear many blessings. Some people turn away from them, not seeing any advantage, and then lay the blame on the shaykh. Overriding the advice of the master, the novice who hopes to curtail the period of his study will only lengthen it. Looking for shortcuts at the beginning of a process will only make it much more difficult later on. If a child knew that he was behaving childishly, he would stop!

> You may think that you've cast off all illusions
> But the idols you create and the pride
> you take in them are still with you!

134

I worry for you at this hour because, unaware of the hardships of separation, you are happily sleeping in the cool shadow of your shaykh's compassion. However, with one wrong move you can lose this mercy, and afterward you can only dream of achieving it again; nor will you ever be able to see your mentor and shaykh again! Without the shaykh willing it, it's impossible to get a glimpse of him, whether in your sleep or while you're awake. Hope is valuable and wise when the possibility of achievement is real; otherwise what's the use?

135

There's no harm in my teachings, and in fact there's plenty to gain, yet in this world there are many people who will be denied even a trace of its goodness. If my conversation does not always appeal to you, nevertheless do not avoid it; respect all that I say so that you may become respectful in turn. But if you choose to be rude and belittle me, you can be certain that your coarseness will reflect back on you, because you're only proving yourself to be blind and useless. Additionally, any respect and service that you may have rendered before would be reevaluated based on your blindness, which misguides others and is only worthy of contempt.

There were ten Sufi companions; one of them fell in love with a young Christian and followed him everywhere, even to the church. The Christian finally confronted him, and reluctantly the Sufi confessed his love. The boy cringed: "It makes me sick to my stomach to encounter someone so vile! How can you even begin to imagine that I would want to come near you?"

The man could think of no other solution than to convert into Christianity and begin wearing the customary silk *zonnâr* belt as the sign. He bid his companions farewell, surprising them all. They wished him well but asked why he was abandoning their company so suddenly. He told them the truth and said that he was on his way to buy the belt. His companions, nine of them in all, decided not to abandon their friend and agreed to convert and wear the *zonnâr* as well, since they were ten bodies in one soul. The young Christian happened to come across them and couldn't help but ask what was going on. They told him about their decision, and as the boy listened he felt a fire kindle in his heart. He tore off his *zonnâr* and exclaimed: "I am the slave of these men who feel such brotherhood and love for each other! I have never seen such fraternity among men."

The young man's father and other relatives gathered around and scolded him for rejecting his religion for the sake of the Sufis' magic, to which he responded: "If you could see what I can see, you too would fall in love with them, perhaps a hundredfold!"

137

If you're fortunate, good advice will polish the mirror of your heart, making it bright and clean. But if you happen to be unfortunate, advice of any sort will only blacken your soul and rust the mirror of your heart beyond recognition!

138

You have repented! But what's the use, you repent every single day!

139

Warriors of God seek death as much as poets seek the verse, the sick seek health, prisoners seek freedom, and children, holidays!

140

Spiritualism can be approached in two different ways, either with an open heart ready to receive revelations from the spirit world or with the mind, through studying mystical texts; both methods require diligence and devotion, refinement and purification. Other than these two, what path is there but the one to hell? God's messengers invite us to acquaint ourselves with them, as we only seem separated from them on the surface. Because we are all connected and part of one another, why should we remain oblivious to the whole? Sadly, though, many of us refuse their invitation and want nothing to do with them, unaware that all the hardships we tolerate, the superficial shelters we hide behind, only create more veils to limit our sight. Indeed, were we to submit to God's messengers, we would easily benefit from revelation after revelation, and discover truth after truth!

141

"They're thorns of society; they must be set to fire!" he exclaimed self-righteously.

I told him: "That's the way of Noah, not Mohammad. Noah would order them to be annihilated all together, but Mohammad's way was to have compassion for those who did him wrong. He considered them ignorant and ultimately worthy of being led to truth."

142

In sleep we dream of scenarios that occur in the real world, but God chooses to reveal them in our sleep because of our delicate nature, until we grow closer to perfection, and then can face them without a veil.

143

I swear that these people who attend schools do so in order to excel in the material world and nothing else! They seek success to improve their social standing. The knowledge they acquire is meant to save them from trouble and not to merely transfer them from one problematic situation to another. Why don't they want to know who they really are, what they're here for, and where they're going? Why don't they ask themselves: What is my essence, what am I doing with myself this very instant, and what awaits me further down the road?

144

Gossip is the most uncouth sin, worse than all other sins put together.

145

A middle-aged man went to the barbershop and asked the barber to separate and cut away his white hairs from the dark to make him look younger for his new bride. The barber took one look at his beard and saw that there were too many white hairs to accomplish the task. He cut the whole beard off and handed the tufts to the man, saying:

"Separate them yourself, I have work to do!"

146

Prayer is like a walking cane for the blind; without it, beneficiaries would never get a scent of the divine.

A follower of the Prophet heard him say that it greatly pleased God when He saw His servants praying sincerely every morning for forty days straight and that He would reward them with great wisdom, which they could then share with others. The man did as he had understood and prayed for forty days, but felt no different; he went to the Prophet and complained that he was not sensing the same depth of insight as another fellow who had been praying, and as the Prophet is never wrong, did he not say that God never gives his subjects a task that they cannot bear? Mohammad said to the man:

"To reveal the purity of one's heart, prayer must be performed with utmost sincerity in order to please God, and only God. Prayer is not to be offered out of temptation or to compete with your fellow man, hoping to boast of your newly acquired wisdom, as you're trying to do now, imitating the other fellow."

148

I am ecstatic that God has given me a friend such as you! I gift my heart to you whether I'm in this world or the next, whether I'm in the pits of the earth or high aloft in the sky. When you can see me and get to know me, why do you then stubbornly dwell on grief? When joy is at hand, why focus on sorrow? If you are with me, how can you be with yourself? And if you are my friend, why are you friends with yourself?

149

Today I heard shaykh Hamid preaching about faith and atheism. I watched him closely and saw that not in a hundred years would he ever know anything about religion or atheism! If he had any wisdom, he would hold his tongue before another shaykh and try to learn something new. He knows what he's already learned quite well and that he can't lose that knowledge, so why not find out if the other person's words might offer something novel, some wisdom that's more complete? It reminds me of the poor *darvish* who only had a slice of bread, and he hid it in his sleeve, telling himself that if he found something better that day, he would let the bread fall to the ground, and it would be free of him, too. Otherwise, while he was still in possession of the one slice, he would hide it well away from strangers' eyes.

150

When a holy person wishes for someone's death, it's not from ill will, but rather he's wishing them death from worldly temptations and their unruly ego!

151

The Koran envelops its messages in myriad veils! To "live off your hard-earned work and the sweat of your brow" means to subsist on spiritual food!

152

Aspiring to ascend to the celestial spheres and indeed hoping to go beyond them shall be of no use to you. You must first open your heart. Why do you think all the prophets and saints worked so hard during their lives? They were in quest of an open heart!

153

A Sufi was crying over the loss of the Prophet and his family, and I was crying for him! Why should anyone cry for the Prophet's family? Why cry for those who have been united with God? If you were conscious of your own state of being, you'd be shedding many more tears for yourself; you'd perhaps have called your entire family, even distant relatives, and together sobbed your hearts out for yourselves!

154

A Sufi had worked hard all his life rendering service to shaykhs and non-Sufis hoping to attain enlightenment. But his time had not yet come!

> For every task there's a promised moment.
> No matter how hard you may work,
> You shall not reap any benefit
> until you've reached that moment of closure.

155

Learned sciences are nothing but veils wrapped around us!

156

God does not change, you do! Sometimes you like to eat bread and grab for it; other times you turn your face away in disgust. Sometimes you're warm toward a friend and he becomes dear to you, but an hour later you may turn cold and find that he no longer appeals to you. Were you to remain steady in your attitude, you too would be constantly loved and cherished.

157

When two people wrestle and fight, the one who's defeated is the real winner, for God has decreed: "I stand with the brokenhearted."

158

Cursing comes easily to some, but the worst curse is: "May all your affairs be delayed till tomorrow." Today has been completely denied them! Poor today, what was its fault not to be counted at all?

159

To think for one hour is infinitely more valuable than to pray for sixty years!

160

Prayer is not valid unless it's performed with a heart that is fully open and present!

161

There are three different types of consciousness. The first is exclusively the home of the devil; the second is the home of angels and the devil, such that when one enters, the other is made to leave. The third, however, is the home of only angels, where the devil can never enter!

162

To lay eyes on the face of my friend, I have to pass through a hundred enemies, but I don't mind and shall oblige.

163

The secret of being charitable is to be so wrapped in sincerity that you have no notion of the pleasure of giving things away!

164

When I like someone, I will be harsh with him, and if he accepts it, I will become his, instantly!

165

One must always try to achieve more, pray more frequently, seek greater knowledge, become a better Sufi, a perfect mystic! Ask more of everything, for whatever exists in the world also exists in man.

166

I have a gem in my heart, and if I ever show it to anyone, he will forsake every friend and companion to gain it!

167

Gradually estrange yourself from the masses. God does not speak with the masses, nor does He belong to them. I don't know what can be gained by keeping their company. What can they save me from or bring me closer to? Do you not possess the same potential as God's messengers? Are you not their follower? Although they were surrounded by the masses, they hardly ever mingled with them, for they belong only to God. Their words must be interpreted and not taken at face value, for often when they say "go," what they really mean is "don't go!"

168

The devil cannot be conceived by the mind; he courses through the veins of man like blood!

169

The hardships that men endure trying to contain the devil will not impair but only strengthen him, because he was conceived by the fires of desire and no light can ever appease him. Nothing can consume evil like the flames of our love!

170

If I reveal myself completely, my task and the ensuing hardship will be greater, because everyone from friends to foes will gather around, and that will prevent me from living the way I need to.

171

In order to build, you must first destroy! You may have great knowledge but still not know the first thing that's best for you. You certainly have the tools, but you don't know where to use them! In order to create, one must first tolerate fire.

172

I never revealed the nature of my prayers to my father, let alone my inner state! He was a kind and generous man, but he wasn't a lover. A good man is one thing and a lover is another. Only a lover can know about the true nature of another lover.

173

If it weren't for Mowlânâ I would never have returned to Konya. Had they brought me the news that my father had risen from the grave and sent me a message to go and see him and come back to Damascus with him, I would never have even considered going!

174

The devil may appear in a common man's blood but never in a *darvish*'s, because he's not the one who speaks, his words come from another sphere, he's dissolved in spirit, he no longer is.

175

At first I did not mingle with religious scholars, only with *darvishes*, for I thought that the former were not conscious of spirituality. Once I became intimately familiar with what true spirituality was and the state in which those *darvishes* lived, I began to prefer the company of the scholars, for they have truly experienced suffering. These *darvishes* lie when they claim to be real ascetics. Tell me, where is their asceticism?

176

It was my parents' fault for raising me with such loving care. If a cat spilled and broke a bowl trying to steal the meat, my father, sitting next to me with his stick by his side, would never hit the animal and would jokingly say: "Look how she's done it again! This is good fortune! We've been spared from evil. Otherwise something bad could've happened to either you, me, or your mother!"

"What is happening to you?" asked my father.

"Nothing has happened to me. Am I mad? Have I torn off someone's clothes? Have I picked a fight with you?"

"Then what is this state I find you in? I know that you are not mad, but I don't understand what you're doing."

"Let me tell you just one thing! The way you are with me is like duck eggs that have been left under a hen. The eggs eventually hatch and the ducklings instinctively walk to the stream. They slide into the water and swim away, as their mother, a domestic hen, only walks alongside them on the bank, without the prospect of ever getting into the water herself. Father, I can now see that the sea has become my carrier, my home! This is the real state of my being. If you are from me and me from you, then come into the sea; otherwise, you can bide your time with the hens in their coop."

178

To remain alone and deny oneself the company of others, to cut off completely from society, is just another way of displaying pride, singling oneself out as an exemplar for others to recognize, which is unacceptable. To deny one's desire for women is also unrealistic; one must favor union with women but one should remain single in spirit. Simply put, to be with people but not of them is indeed to adhere to the Prophet's decree.

179

He says he doesn't wish to hurt even a mosquito, yet he defies God and His subjects and doesn't bat an eye!

180

"Was he a mystic?"

"His father was a mystic and a learned man."

"I didn't ask about his father; I want to know about him."

"His father was very knowledgeable."

"Don't you hear what I'm asking you?"

"I can hear you but you don't hear me! I'm not deaf; I can hear what you're asking!"

181

When I was young I was asked, why was I so glum? Did I desire better clothing or perhaps more money? I replied that I wished they would take away the little clothing I had and return to me that which truly belongs to me!

182

Each person commits a transgression worthy only of him; for one, it's to be a rogue and commit debauchery, while for another it's to be absent before God!

183

I'm not incompetent; I am a problem solver! I find solutions to the problems of the world, not my own!

184

There lived a shaykh in Baghdad who was performing his forty-day retreat. On the eve of Eid, he heard a voice not of this world telling him that he'd been bestowed with the breath of Jesus and that he should go out among the masses and offer what he'd been graced with. The shaykh descended into deep thought, wondering, what could the purpose of this revelation possibly be? Was it a test perhaps? A second call came more vehemently, telling him to cast off his doubts and go out into the crowd, as he had been bestowed with the breath of Jesus. He waited a little longer, thinking that further reflection might help him understand the purpose of this demand. For a third time the call came, even louder and stronger than before:

"I have bestowed the breath of Jesus unto you; go out immediately!"

The shaykh reluctantly went out of his retreat and began walking among the crowds of Baghdad. He noticed a halva seller who had shaped the sweets into birds, and he thought he might experiment here. Much to the surprise of the crowd, who wondered what the shaykh could possibly want with sweets as he was supposed to be above such temptations, he beckoned the halva maker. The shaykh took one bird-shaped halva from the tray and laid it on his palm, blowing his breath onto it. Instantly the bird grew flesh, skin, bones, and feathers and flew away.

Astounded, the crowd gathered around, and the shaykh blew life into several more birds. Eventually he grew tired of the crowd's pressing numbers, their constant prostrations and amazement at his acts of wonder, and began walking away toward the desert. The crowd would not leave him alone and followed him closely. No matter how many times he asked them to leave him alone, saying that he had a private affair to tend to, they would not listen. He continued walking in the desert for a long while asking God why He had inflicted such imprisonment on him: what lesson was God trying to teach him? Finally, he had a revelation, telling him to do something to offend the men following him, thus encouraging them to disappear. So the shaykh loudly passed wind. Everyone looked at each other shaking their heads in disgust, and they quickly returned to town, except one man who remained behind and would not go away. The shaykh was curious to discover why he hadn't joined with the others and followed them but was initially too embarrassed to ask. He was in fact in awe of the man's devotion, and finally he overcame his nerves and asked him. The man confessed:

"I did not follow you because of your first blowing of wind so why should I leave because of the second? To me, the second wind was even better than the first because it relieved your precious being of discomfort, whereas the first only brought you hardship and suffering!"

185

I possess reins that no one dares to touch, except for the Prophet, but even he thinks twice before taking them and would never try when I'm in the throes of ecstasy!

186

One must admit to one's wrongdoing once and for all and not constantly agonize and obsess over it. Our inner regulator must externalize our sin and remove it from our consciousness so that we do not consume ourselves over it and render ourselves incapable of dealing with our real work. A cat may try to steal a piece of meat from my table, but if I concentrate on chasing the cat, I'll miss out on eating the meat!

187

The purpose of conversing with people is to call them to action! Before their eyes there's a veil, before their hearts there's a veil, and I shall lift these veils once and for all.

188

When Hallaj was to be hanged, Baghdad's religious leaders ordered every citizen of the city, including all his friends, to throw a stone at him. While most people threw stones and rocks, his friends threw flowers. When he began to moan and sigh at the flowers, his persecutors, surprised that he had not made a single sound until then, asked him, why was he moaning now?

"Don't you know that unkindness by a friend is so much more hurtful than that of one's enemy?"

189

Every time you experience joy and rapture, know that inevitably they herald the eventual arrival of sorrow and grief. Joy promises pending grief; every opening of the heart trumpets its subsequent closure. How wonderful to find pleasure in nature, like being enchanted by ethereal blossoms—for a while they steal your heart, but after an hour you can't bear their stench. Sadness and frustration overwhelm you until you want to flee even from your own skin! You reach out and hang onto anything to keep your sanity, so you delve into literature and art, even playing games with children. However, this cycle of joy and sorrow soon repeats itself; the blossoms again let loose their thorns, leaving you stranded with your fear and solitude. Push away these forever changing colors in your life so that you may see another life, a spiritual life that is not dependent on joy or sorrow.

190

This house called the world is a reflection of the human body, and the body is a reflection of that other world.

191

You might, at some point, have a thought and then become upset by it. That thought gives birth to another thought and then yet another one, and so on and so forth. Repeat to yourself three times: "Go away, thought!" and if it doesn't comply, then you yourself must go away! Whatever has caused your anxiety, stop doing it, don't eat it or drink it, don't even touch it or go near it!

192

A man rushed to me bearing awful news, telling of the imminent arrival of the murderous Tatars. I asked him:

"Aren't you ashamed of yourself! You, who until now has boasted about what an artful duck you are, how can you now fear a storm? How strange to encounter a duck seeking a ship for rescue!"

193

Two friends who had been together for a long time came to serve a shaykh. His first question for them was, how long had they been together as confidants?

"Many years," they responded.

"Have you ever had a disagreement?" he asked.

"No, never! We've only ever agreed with each other."

"You must know that you've lived in discord all this time! Surely you each must have noticed some objectionable act by the other that made you upset."

"Yes, that's true."

"And you never mentioned to the other that you were hurt by that act, out of fear, didn't you?"

"Yes, you're right!" they admitted shamefully.

194

There is a *darvish* who's considered humble and poor when it comes to food, and there's another *darvish* who is humble and poor when it comes to God! To be a *darvish* has nothing to do with having a torn garment on one's back!

195

A man was wailing that his livelihood had been plundered. I told him a story:

Once upon a time there was a grocer who had an Indian manservant. The grocer had the bad habit of skimming a little off each batch of condensed oil or honey that he sold. The servant did not like what he saw but kept it to himself, until one day a large container of syrup broke open and the contents all went to waste. The servant sighed to himself, thinking, when you unlawfully take one spoonful away at a time you'll eventually lose the whole container in one go! Don't do evil; it will fall back on you. Don't dig a hole; you're bound to be the first one to fall into it!

196

"Let's go perform the prayer for the dead, so-and-so has passed away," one Sufi said to another.

The other Sufi did not feel like going and said instead: "May God rest his soul in peace."

The prayer for the dead is not more than this: "May God rest him in peace"! When someone is unfamiliar with the essence, he trifles with the trivialities instead!

197

Many great men lost their affection for me because they thought I was after their money. I wasn't; I was after getting those idiots to *part* with their money! They were great shaykhs and dignitaries, and what could I possibly want with shaykhs and so-called great men? I want *you* the way you are! I want *need,* I want *hunger,* and I want *thirst!* Clear water seeks the thirsty because it is generous and kind.

198

There was a man who claimed to be my friend; like a true *morīd,* he claimed that we were two bodies in one soul. One day I tested him:

"You have large amount of savings; go and find me a beautiful wife, and if her family asks for 300 dirhams for her dowry, offer them 400 instead!"

Shocked, he fled, never to be seen again.

199

Let's go to the whorehouse to pay a visit to those poor souls; hasn't God created them too? Never mind if they're sinful, let's go and see them anyway; and let's go to the church as well, and see the people there too. Not many can tolerate my work; what I do is not for hypocrites!

200

A man was complaining about his child's behavior; I couldn't help but tell him not to be too bothered, that the child's future will be all right, that he's only a child now and does childish things, but that doesn't reflect his essence. Remember that the unripe grape and the apricot are bitterly sour; the child is like the unripe grape because he's still young, not because he's evil inside! There are those, however, who are indeed sour and hard as rock inside who will never ripen sweet. The sour grape must be exposed to the sun!

201

To say "Allâh o Akbar," "God is Great," in prayer is to sacrifice the ego! While you still harbor pride and imagine yourself to exist, you need to repeat "God is Great" indefinitely.

202

Shaykh Mahmood, better known as Ibn Arabi, prayed constantly and claimed to be a follower of Islam. I learned a lot from him, but nothing like what I've learned from you, Mowlânâ! It's like comparing pebbles with pearls!

203

One man exerts himself excessively in order to show off, and the other plots a hundred times to conceal himself!

204

A *darvish* owns nothing and nothing owns a *darvish*!

205

It is in childhood that one needs to nourish the proper attitude so that one can achieve results much faster later on. A branch can be treated much easier when still young than when it becomes dry and unbendable.

206

If I don't test him, he will never know who he is! Didn't you see how those people who claimed to be completely devoted and offered many sacrifices reacted when I began to test the extent of their belief? Did you notice how I exposed them, so you could see how they look without their masks? The ones who pretend to sacrifice their lives for you—the minute you ask them for a penny, they lose their minds, their best intentions evaporate, and they don't know what to do with themselves! I tested them so they could face a little bit of their true selves.

207

The mind is feeble; you can't expect much from it. It may guide you to the door but never inside the house!

208

Each person experiences a different inner state: the preacher at the pulpit is in one state, the Koranic teacher on his stool is in a different state, their audiences are in another state, the shaykh is aware of his own state of mind and the *morīd* of his, while the lover and the beloved each experience different inner states of being. I, however, hail the blind man who, in his totally downtrodden state, is unaware of his blindness!

209

I have the power to prevent my grief from affecting anyone, for no one can tolerate it and it will kill them. They can't tolerate my joy, so how could they possibly dream of tolerating my sorrow?

210

A man once complained about the people he encountered in this world, and he was told:

"Life is all fun and games for the powerful and wealthy; for children, though, their play is not a game: it's serious business, a duty and a responsibility—it's what they do. If you cannot bear to joke and play, then don't. But if you do choose to indulge in this manner, then go on and play, enjoy yourself! For the sweetness of games is all about laughter, not tears."

211

The mind that belongs to this world speaks through the mouth, while the mind that is of the spirit world speaks from the heart!

212

What is reflection? Is it to look at the past, to look at those who came before us, to see if they were thankful for what was imparted to them and whether they had benefited from it or not? Or is it to look at the future and imagine how a piece of advice may affect someone in the end? Only someone who's not bound by the affections of the world can look purposefully at the past and the future, for had he been affected by them, he would already have been blinded.

213

When someone badmouths your friend and accuses him of jealousy, whether it's your own inner voice or the voice of another person, you should know for certain that the accusatory voice himself is the jealous one! Indeed, he's boiling inside with envy!

214

Question: "The imam who was leading the prayer could not control his eyes, which wandered left and right constantly. Isn't his prayer annulled?"

Answer: "Both of their prayers are annulled."

"I'm asking about the imam's prayer; who's the second person?"

"The first one is the imam, whose gaze is jumping here and there disturbing those present, and the second one is the follower, who has become the imam's delegate, looking out for him instead of concentrating on his own praying!"

215

Those who go on the defensive with God's messengers believing that they're being unfairly treated are in fact being regarded too kindly. The messengers detach their hearts from men, because they feel the pain of all men, and this is a heavy burden on them. When they let go of people, it's as if the weight of a mountain had been lifted off their shoulders. They don't know how to become anyone's enemy, and to lay the weight of a mountain on their shoulders—in other words, to oblige them to increase their love and affection for men—is in fact enmity. To lift the thoughts and the love of men, though, is to do the messengers an immense favor.

216

I am surprised at the hadith, which claims that the world is the prison of the pious and the grave is their safe house and paradise—their eternal resting place—while, for the infidel, the world is his paradise, the grave is a torture chamber, and hell is his throne! I personally have seen nothing but joy, greatness, and abundance in this life!

217

When I speak to a crowd, you must recognize what I'm saying to you personally and not fabricate words I haven't spoken. When you listen to me, that shows the strength of your belief in me. For why should your friend not reiterate his thoughts for you until you grasp them well? And if you don't understand the second time around, why not ask again? If you are afraid, then the devil has penetrated your thoughts and tricked you to forsake your friend, luring you toward the lonesome desert with his familiar song. Although he will never be able to separate you from me, still one must be diligent at all times.

218

What is a secret? A secret depends on the listener, who must recognize it amid all the superficial discourse that goes on!

219

God has decreed that each of us will have insight to specific aspects of life and not others; for example, one person may only comprehend the benefits of being a goldsmith, while another knows only about alchemy, a group of others know about religious jurisprudence, and yet another will know about magic and trickery. Meanwhile, one group realizes God's light and the comfort of the afterlife, while another group will know of love, beauty, and sex, and yet another group will intimately know of angels and celestial beings. Each person sees the world from his own perspective and has a different view of life from everyone else's.

220

Retreats are a novelty in Mohammad's religion! He never did a forty-day retreat, which is popular in Sufi groups. This custom belongs to Moses!

221

What a life! To be no one's servant nor to be anyone's master! Honestly, what a life the Sufi leads!

222

We must be grateful for the pious, because they're not infidels, and we must be thankful for the infidels, for they're not hypocrites!

223

There are two types of hypocrisy: one is obvious to all, and may it be kept far and away from our loved ones and ourselves. Then there's the other type, which is hidden: one must take a leap of faith to cut it at the root, for it lies in our own nature.

224

Pull the cotton wool out of your ears so that you never become a prisoner of words or a victim of life's affectations. Open your eyes and your ears; become conscious of the bargaining that's hashed out in your own soul.

225

How can one take warring people into one's confidence? By making them repudiate their wars and feuds of course! War derives from temptation and greed; you'll see this at the core of every conflict.

226

Your mentor is love
who will show you what to do
in the language of love.

227

"Let me tell you about a magic trick, not witchcraft, with
which you can capture free men and bring them into
your service such that it will not cost you a single dirham
or dinar," proclaimed the Prophet.

"Tell us, tell us," the men hailed.

"Be gentle in your acts, be gentle with your words!"

228

The purpose of telling a story is not to lift one's boredom
but mostly to lift one's ignorance.

The Prophet's act of submission and devotion was to delve deep into his own consciousness, an act of the heart and a service rendered to the heart; it involved his total surrender, his dissolution into the Beloved. He knew, however, that this approach would not be right for everyone, that very few would experience being so immersed in the love of God, so he decreed certain practices: prayer five times every day, fasting for thirty days, and the pilgrimage to Mecca! This was done in the hope that, by adhering to these practices, the masses would not feel abandoned and in fact would feel that they had a higher stature among their friends and could hope to be free one day and perhaps even savor a taste of what it means to lose oneself in love. Otherwise, what need does God have of our hunger or of our persisting with vigorous religious rituals?

230

Most shaykhs today are thieves of our faith. They are like mice gnawing away at the foundation of our house. There are also those—darling subjects—who play the role of cats, responsible for clearing out the mice. Even if a hundred thousand mice gathered together, they'd be unable to look the cat in the eyes, out of awe. The cat is sure of herself and controls her ego while raising fear in the mice. If the mice dared to work together, they might overcome the cat, perhaps losing a few along the way: while the cat is busy catching one mouse, another might jump at her, while another could rush at her eye and puncture it. It's fear, though, that prevents the mice from gathering together their strength and acting in unison.

231

The sura in the Koran about the Kaaba that says, "There is light inside this house, and when you enter it you will be safe at all times," is no doubt referring to the quality of the heart: while the dangers of temptation lie everywhere without, inside there's eternal safety.

232

To differentiate between friend and foe
One must live at least twice!
Enemies with friendly faces are rampant,
But where is the friend whose heart bleeds for you?

233

When people seek peace, they say things that will please the other party, enticing him into friendship and amity. One might apologize for one's past behavior and harsh words, blaming the devil's mischief. One might even plead with God and confess to one's sins, regretting each word or act that may have hurt the other person. Thus, every word and every action should reflect the wish to make peace with one's friend.

234

To "live twice" refers to a person who has not succumbed to his ego but instead has found a new and fresh life, where he can look with God's light in his eyes and know instantly who is a friend and who isn't. He will express anger at the appropriate time, and likewise his kindness will be well deserved, and both shall be true.

235

My heart was settled on you from the very beginning, but I could tell from our conversation that you were not yet ready to hear my secrets. You were not in the right state of mind then, but now is the hour!

236

One day a king was riding along with his men in the countryside. As they approached a village, the troops rode ahead to clear the pedestrians out of the way. Suddenly, unnoticed by the others, a poverty-stricken man jumped before the king and began to curse him. The king didn't mention this to his retainers, because if they found out they would shred the man to pieces. He then changed the course of his route, surprising his men, who asked him for the reason. He simply told them that he had changed his mind.

Why should the king get angry with a homeless beggar? Were they of the same essence? A king will go to war only with those who are worthy of a fight.

237

There is no one alive who doesn't entertain a degree of selfishness and egotism!

238

People all love to hear the word, "Bravo!" They will fall over themselves to be told: "Well done!"

239

When you feel the full presence of a friend who's far away, how will it feel when he's sitting right in front of you?

240

If you're Mowlânâ's friend, then don't buy his son Alâeddin a chess set, as this is the time for his education, and he needs his sleep at night. He should be studying every day, even if it's to learn only one line. If he hears me saying this, he'll be upset with me because he believes that I force him to work unnecessarily. That's why he's also at war with God, believing Him to be promoting needless work as well. The moment he gets a whiff of work, he takes flight! How strange that some love to waste their little precious time!

241

"I'm burning, I can't tolerate this torture!" he cries, but the master tells him that's precisely why he's keeping him. The man implores:

"My lord, have pity, you are setting me on fire; what do you want with this poor servant?"

"It is this burning that I want to see!" he's told.

This is similar to the story in which the lover breaks a pot of ink; his beloved asks him why, and he responds:

"So that I can hear you ask me why!"

The wisdom of the story lies in the act of shedding tears in order to encourage the expression of kindness and love. Unless you cry, unless you feel pain, the sea of blessing shall not be opened to you. Until the infant cries, the mother, despite her unconditional love, will not attempt to feed him.

242

All during Ramadan, at least a hundred people asked me to join them in breaking the fast. I sent most of them away and asked the caravansary owner to tell anyone else who may come that others have already taken me away with them.

243

My heart is no one's treasury but God's! Why should I allow idiots to roam free inside? I'll throw them all out in no time!

244

My heart has no concept of itself; it finds its nourishment from another place. It is in fact nourished on itself.

245

A group of men kept inviting me, and I kept conjuring excuses to avoid them, for they were Muslim only on the outside and infidels inside! I used to go to church and found many infidels who became my friends; infidels on the outside but true Muslims inside! One day I asked them to bring me something to eat. They were overjoyed and, with great appreciation, brought food and broke their fast with me! They had been fasting secretly!

246

When you hurt me, you will be hurting Mowlânâ in turn.

247

Each verse of the Koran contains a message; each is a love letter.

248

Do you really think God cares if you went to the pleasure house?

249

What can the unbelieving infidel say other than his regular blasphemy? The faithful talk about faith, while the unbelievers blaspheme. Garbage in, garbage out!

250

A tailor who wants to try his hand at ironmongery will scorch his beard, unless he goes to the ironmonger and asks to be taught properly; then he'll keep his beard safe, like the ironmonger's.

251

You can spend a lot of money on your groceries, but if you don't add a little salt to your food, it will be inedible. You can't just talk about salt; you must actually use it.

252

They expose their ignorance when they begin to speak, making loud declarations but demonstrating only their own unsightliness! Why don't they just give it up and make room for a competent speaker to talk? And when he begins, they must remain silent until he's come to the end of his speech. Your place is that of a listener. When you yourself attempt to speak, you'll only push your goal farther into the distance.

253

At first, the fish was chasing the water, and now it's the water that chases the fish everywhere it goes!

254

Meat, wine, and melon have a quality such that when they are consumed by a healthy body, they serve to reinforce health, but if they are consumed by a diseased body, they will befriend illness. That's the reason why it's recommended to avoid eating meat altogether.

255

A man rushed to the mosque to perform his prayer, but the group prayer was over:

"Are they finished?" he gasped.

"Yes," said one of the men.

Upset to have missed out, the man sighed remorsefully. Hearing his deep sigh, the other man begged him:

"I'll donate to you all of my life's prayers; just give me that sigh!"

256

Your companion must be better than you, so he can lift you up and make you better, too.

257

I have filled my cup, but I cannot drink it; I can't pour it out either! My heart doesn't allow me to let you go, as I've done with the others!

258

Those who squander their possessions are the companions of the devil. They throw away not only their money but also their lives, their eternal asset. Let's just say for argument's sake that there's no doomsday or resurrection; still, how can one hide this gem of a life under a rock and let it simply go to waste?

259

When you're in the midst of worship, what business have you with slander and backbiting? When your mouth is filled with sugar, what business does vinegar have there too? Could it be that perhaps your mouth was always filled with the sourness of vinegar?

260

To understand the messengers of God is much more difficult than to understand God! One can conceive that every object has been crafted by an expert hand, that it hasn't just appeared on its own. But the messengers, whom you consider similar to yourself on the inside and out, have a different story beyond your imagination. To conceive of the craftsman is not so difficult, but how are we to understand how He truly is, how glorious is His glory, and how His infinity can be conceived? These insights are known only by His messengers, and you expect them to just share them with you so candidly?

261

The sura that says, "Those who exert their efforts on Our path shall be guided back to Us," should actually be read in reverse: "When you see people exerting their efforts on Our path, you must know that they are being guided by Us!"

262

When they hurt me, I only get stronger; I become even greater than I already am!

263

Until your sleep becomes like your wakefulness, do not fall asleep! How could it be that God is awake while his servant sleeps? Be such that the hours in which you sleep are exactly the same as your waking hours.

264

You complain that since you've eaten a particular food, you've been constantly ill and suffering, unable to hear or even speak properly. Have you ever come across something that's supposed to strengthen you to instead be bad for you and cause you such pain? What else remains if one can't enjoy the normal things in life? Don't eat something that later on might make you say, "I wish I hadn't touched it; I was so well before! How I regret having eaten it!"

265

When God is happy with you, angels will turn to face you. When you have embraced the Gardener, the whole garden is yours to pick from at your delight!

266

Not all weddings are the same; this too is a
    wedding!
I sigh in grief when I'm separated from my love,
I scream in pain when I hear my beloved's goodbye;
How much sweeter will be my death,
having endured these two calamities in life!

267

A wine merchant was selling his wine when a man looked
at him and wondered:

"How strange! You're selling wine? What could you
possibly buy that's better?"

268

An act of kindness by a judge is infinitely more valuable
than the legal testimony of two witnesses.

269

There is no shortage of thinking. You come up with a
thought and make it your mask. From the first thought
you are led to the next and the next, but none with any
value.

270

"Bring out the gold you're hiding away."

"I am nothing!"

"Bring that 'nothingness' then."

"First, why don't you show your own 'being'?"

"'Being' seeks 'nothingness'!"

"I'm already in tears, I need someone to cheer me up!"

Become such a drunk that you can experience total consciousness!

271

People are hypocrites; the more scholarly they are, the more they merely copycat each other! Some try to imitate the state of the heart of others, while some try to copy others' joy. Meanwhile, some attempt to imitate the Prophet and others try to imitate God by repeating His words. Yet another group does not copy God or repeat His words; they only speak of themselves!

272

My only intention in saying "temple of idols" and "Kaaba" is to call your name! I whisper the words "idol-temple" just to remind myself of you and the majesty of your face. I say the word "idol" because of its meaning, but without a beloved there can be no idol.

273

The celestial spheres and everyone inhabiting them will rise to their feet to dance when one perfect man begins to whirl!

274

Man has been created for a purpose—to find his origin, where he comes from. His outer and inner senses have been gifted to him as tools for finding this wisdom. When he uses them for other purposes, he will feel unsafe and be unable to enjoy his life. Even if he spends most of his time studying, which in itself is a noble cause, he'll still be denied his original purpose in life.

275

Some people are the scribes of divine messages, and some are the recipients. Take a leap so that you are both the receiver and the scribe of messages meant for you.

276

If you see me as stale, it's because you've become stale! See me only as fresh and new, for I never grow old. Try not to give in to advancing age, and if you do feel old, search for the reason. Think whom you've been socializing with. Lay the blame on yourself, and revitalize your yearning. I am always new and do not need your approval, for I'm perpetually blessed.

277

I do not obey and bow to the Koran because it's God's words but because the Prophet Mohammad has uttered those words!

278

Love and conviction make one brave and push all looming fears to the far horizon.

279

A Greek man, a non-Muslim, who walks through this door and sees me may begin to believe. He will learn much more from me than from these so-called shaykhs who are so full of themselves and have squandered their biggest asset, which is their need for Spirit; they have turned themselves into vagabonds on earth.

280

When I busy myself with talk, the meaning comes chasing me!

281

To pray, to practice asceticism, and to render service should not solely be to gain glory but to give sincerely out of devotion, without the expectation of any return.

282

When you walk the spiritual path and you work hard being true to your convictions, then why don't you share your purpose with another person as well? Why do you leave your friend to languish in his slumber? Are you an imposter, a hypocrite?

283

Trees are grown for their crop, but if they don't bear fruit, then perhaps it's best to cut them and burn them for heat they can generate.

284

Two people sit before each other; one has no trace of an eye disease, nothing to hamper his vision, yet he sees nothing, while the other sees all!

285

A patient who seeks a physician's help should not be occupied with anything other than his health. If a thirsty person desperate to find drinking water is offered sweet halva and accepts it, then his claim to thirst has been fictitious. A hungry person who claims to be famished but is offered drinking water instead and drinks it is also being deceptive.

286

When you meet someone who has a broad and all-encompassing personality, who speaks with an open mind and practices great patience, who prays for everyone in the world and encourages you to open up your heart and lifts your spirit out of this superficial, narrow world, he's an angel from paradise. And if you come by a person whose talk incites you to close your heart, if you feel his restricted view of the world turning you cold and disengaging you from life, exactly the opposite of the angelic person, he's evil and belongs in hell. When you have understood this concept, when it becomes consonant with your being, then no shaykh in the world can steal your love.

287

A hundred years of education is nothing compared with one moment spent with God!

288

When Aristotle and his followers said that if everyone were like them, then there would be no need for prophets, they spoke nonsense!

289

I am in total control of my ego! If I were offered a table full of exquisitely prepared dishes and sweets that others would give their right arm for, I would never touch them. I would not even desire them. Keeping my appetite under control, I prefer a portion of barley bread when it's time to eat, which is much healthier than extravagant offerings of biryani with grilled meats.

290

Who could ever survive in your love but me?
Who plants seeds in salt fields but me?
I shall relentlessly gossip about you
    to friends and foe
So no one will love you but me!

291

An ascetic who lives in a cave in the mountains is a mountain man and no longer a thinking human, for if he were, he'd be living among men who are intelligent and worthy of God's wisdom. What business do men have living in a cave? If man were made of mud, then he would be attracted to rocks, but what can a flesh-and-blood man want with rocks? Do not go into *khalvat* or seclusion and solitude; remain an individual, present but detached, in the midst of a crowd; and remember that the Prophet says: "In Islam there is no monasticism."

292

God's world is infinite, an endless opening of the Spirit that is extremely difficult for some to comprehend and at the same time much too easy an experience for others, so effortless in fact that they puzzle over why people even choose to talk about it!

293

Great secrets are hidden in the lines of jokes and tall tales.

294

I have only one friend in the entire world; how can I deny him his wish? You are not my friends; how could you even think that you might be? It's only because of Mowlânâ that you may hear a few sentences, otherwise no one would hear a word from me. Did you ever hear me speak with anyone before or part with any secrets? When I speak to common men, listen carefully, because my words are secrets. Whoever belittles the advice I impart to laymen, thinking that it is mere superficial rambling and too simple for serious consideration, shall not benefit in the least from my thoughts or from me. It is indeed in my conversations with regular folks that I reveal most of my cherished secrets.

295

You could lay out a hundred thousand dirhams as a gift before me, or even offer me a castle filled with gold, but unless I see a light in your brow and detect yearning in your heart, you will be the same for me as a mound of feces!

296

I told Mowlânâ straightforwardly that these people do not understand what I say. God has not ordered me to speak of mundane subjects. I'm only to tell the absolute truth, which would be too difficult for them to comprehend. With them, I will have to speak of an overlapping truth in order to conceal the original one, and so on and so forth until each sentence becomes a cover-up for the one before.

297

Inanimate objects experience separation and union too—only we can't hear their sighs!

298

The world of Spirit is vast, unlimited in fact, but you have restricted it to a tiny package because that's all your mind can perceive. Thus you have boxed in the creator of the mind in your own negligible mind!

299

When someone begins to believe in our faith, he in fact rejects his ego and its desires. We say that he thus "dies," meaning that darkness no longer prevails, and this gift will henceforth be constant and unperturbed.

300

We are a quiet pool of water hidden under a cover of hay; as long as the water gently circulates beneath, the hay is unconscious of it until suddenly it's pushed up in the air and the water instantly begins to flow steadily outward.

301

The word is an attribute. When He comes into speech, He hides in the words as a way to reach His audience. Unless He veils Himself in words, how else can the attribute reach out to those who are themselves living behind veils? In the end it's up to Him to either keep the veils or push them aside.

302

In reality, no one can accompany me, for I am *lâobâli!* Being separated from Mowlânâ does not bother me, nor does union with him bring me much pleasure, for my joy comes from within me, as does my pain! It's not easy to live with someone like me.

303

When water is stirred in with various unclean agents, what is to prevent the thirsty from nevertheless approaching? There is one variety of water that cannot tolerate impurity, and thus it repels all vile additives. And there's yet another kind of water that, no matter what filthy elements are mixed in, its purity is never diluted.

304

When you repent every day and then break your promise every day, you make yourself a figure of mockery and easy prey for the devil.

305

The meaning of words is like water contained in a pitcher; without the pitcher, one can't grasp the water. I needed to understand the meaning garbed in Arabic words, that was my only intention in learning the Arabic language.

306

The "path" lies beyond the reality of being a *pīr* or a *morīd*, a master or a follower!

307

I needed someone of my own caliber to make a Mecca of him and turn to him, for I had become weary of myself!

308

Hearts are sealed, tongues are sealed, and ears are sealed. If you detect a sliver of light peeping through, be grateful and give thanks—perhaps the light might increase. Pray to be shown everything as it is, and when you are grateful, God will increase His benevolence toward you.

309

I'm in love with the flowing curls of your hair
Because they're in love with my crazy heart!

310

A man asked a pharmacist to give him a cure for baldness. The bald pharmacist took one look at him and sneered:
"If I had a cure, don't you think I'd cure myself first?!"

311

It's not often that friends find each other and bring such peace to one another.

> Years are needed under the sun
> to turn a rough stone into a gem in Badakhshan
> or into an agate in Yemen.
> Months are needed under the earth
> for a cotton seed to be transformed into muslin
> to wrap around a corpse or to veil
> the body of a beautiful lady.

312

You can see everyone in yourself including Moses, Jesus, Abraham, Noah, Adam, Eve, Kidr, Elias, the Antichrist, and even Asiya, the pharaoh's wife! Knowing this, what possible value can the limited earth and sky have, when you are the infinite universe? Remember what God said:

"Neither the sky nor the earth can contain me; other than the heart of my devoted servant, nothing can contain me!"